Advance praise for the book

'In the emerging knowledge society 2.0, whose contours will be continually transformed by the increasing power of Generative AI, Gopalakrishnan and Bhattacharyya offer deep insights through a wide spectrum of examples on how organisations to be relevant must cultivate the spirit of "eternal youthfulness" through curiosity, creativity and compassion. Given the perennial nature of these messages, I believe this book will retain its relevance for many generations.'

Partha S. Ghosh
Chairman, The Boston Pledge; Mentor to CEOs; Professor of Practice, Tufts University; Founder of Academy of Leadership, IIT Kharagpur; Ex-Partner, McKinsey & Company

'Corporate transformation occupies centre stage in boardrooms today. Given the scale and scope of the multifarious challenges being faced by businesses currently, this should not be surprising. In fact, transformation is now a continuum and no longer episodic. *Embrace the Future* – a very apt title – is undoubtedly a timely book as it describes in detail the elements which go into making a successful transformation. I can vouch for these factors as I was deeply involved in the transformation of Tata Steel, one of the companies covered in the book. The authors rightly emphasise the often-overlooked importance of focusing on an organisation's culture and values while undertaking the task of organisational transformation.'

Ishaat Hussain
Independent Board Director; Former Director, Finance, Tata Sons

'"If it ain't broke, don't fix it," taught de Bono. Tinker, cost-cut and buy time as a "filtered" CEO, and you lead your company to an early grave. Drawing on illustrations from history, nature, medicine, religion and their own formidable experience, the two authors make a powerful case for continual (not episodic) transformation, with an inextricably wound Yin and Yang helix of heart and mind, predicated of purpose and a targeted future: how Amazon ate Sears and stunted Walmart; how London's black cabs bounced back from the Uber onslaught; and how a crucible of technological, societal and business system changes can ward off corporate mortality. Start by reading the epilogue.'

Nihal Kaviratne CBE
Former Board Member of DBS Bank and sixteen other corporates

'At long last, here's a book that gets the process of organisational transformation right! We've been misled for years by detailed, step-by-step how-to manuals that assumed "change management" was a process with clear starting and finishing points. In truth, there is no universal "change management" template, and no starting and finishing points to the process of change. In fact, change is the only constant in today's turbulent business environment. Thus, by necessity, managing continual organisational change has become the primary role and responsibility of leadership. In these pages, the authors draw on their years of practical experience at Unilever and Tata to offer invaluable insights and wisdom to those who wish to master the art of leading change.'

James O'Toole
Author of *The Enlightened Capitalists*

EMBRACE THE FUTURE

EMBRACE THE FUTURE

The Soft Science of Business Transformation

R. GOPALAKRISHNAN
HRISHI BHATTACHARYYA

Foreword by Nitin Paranjpe

BLOOMSBURY
NEW DELHI · LONDON · OXFORD · NEW YORK · SYDNEY

BLOOMSBURY INDIA
Bloomsbury Publishing India Pvt. Ltd
Second Floor, LSC Building No. 4, DDA Complex, Pocket C – 6 & 7,
Vasant Kunj, New Delhi, 110070

BLOOMSBURY, BLOOMSBURY INDIA and the Diana logo
are trademarks of Bloomsbury Publishing Plc

First published in 2024
This edition published 2024

Copyright © R. Gopalakrishnan and Hrishikesh Bhattacharyya, 2024
Foreword copyright © Nitin Paranjpe, 2024

R. Gopalakrishnan and Hrishikesh Bhattacharyya have asserted their
right under the Indian Copyright Act to be identified as the Authors of this work

All rights reserved. No part of this publication may be reproduced or transmitted in
any form or by any means, electronic or mechanical, including photocopying,
recording or any information storage or retrieval system, without the prior
permission in writing from the publishers

This book is solely the responsibility of the authors and the publisher has had no
role in the creation of the content and does not have responsibility for anything
defamatory or libellous or objectionable

Bloomsbury Publishing Plc does not have any control over, or responsibility for,
any third-party websites referred to or in this book. All internet addresses given in this
book were correct at the time of going to press. The author and publisher regret any
inconvenience caused if addresses have changed or sites have ceased to exist, but can
accept no responsibility for any such changes

ISBN: HB: 978-93-56403-53-6; e-ISBN: 978-93-56403-52-9
2 4 6 8 10 9 7 5 3 1

Typeset in Baskerville MT Std by Manipal Technologies Limited
Printed and bound in India

To find out more about our authors and books visit www.bloomsbury.com and sign
up for our newsletters

Contents

Foreword by Nitin Paranjpe   ix

1   Heart plus Mind   1

PART 1: THE SOFT ASPECTS OF TRANSFORMATION

2   Software: Transformation as Art   19
3   Pain: Endurance and Inevitability   57
4   Leadership: Followers and Leaders   69
5   Review: Checks and Balances   86
6   Long Life: Continual Renewal   94

PART 2: THE STRATEGIC ASPECTS OF TRANSFORMATION

7   Hindsight for Foresight   123
8   Future: How Much Will It Be Like the Past?   128
9   Strategy: Creating a Transformational One   148
10   Transformation: Ambition to Strategy   166
11   Assumptions: How to Challenge Them   188
12   Reinvent or Perish: Three Examples   208

Epilogue   227

Acknowledgements   235
Notes   236
Index   240
About the Authors   248

Foreword

In a world where change is the only constant, the ability to adapt and transform has become a hallmark of successful businesses and visionary leaders. It is with great pleasure and admiration that I introduce the insightful and enlightening book *Embrace the Future: The Soft Science of Business Transformation* by Mr Gopalakrishnan (Gopal) and Mr Bhattacharyya (Hrishi).

Before proceeding, full disclosure: when I began my journey as a young trainee, Gopal and Hrishi were both senior leaders at Hindustan Lever Limited (HLL). Each, in his own way, had a big influence on young professionals like me in our formative years. It would not be an overstatement to say that I grew up in awe of them and continue to have the deepest respect for them as professionals and human beings. Therefore, being asked to write a foreword for their new book is truly an honour for me.

Despite my admitted bias for the above reasons, I do think this book is special.

Special because it draws on their extensive first-hand experiences spanning across a hundred-plus years, leading transformational journeys in India and beyond. Gopal and Hrishi generously share their personal insights on various global transformation case studies, making this book an extensive library in itself for individuals leading any form of change. The real-world examples and practical frameworks offer a deep understanding of the challenges and triumphs of transformational journeys. The candid accounts of both their successes and failures serve as powerful teaching moments, enabling readers to learn from the experiences of others and avoid common pitfalls. Written in an easy-to-read style, without excessive business jargon, the wisdom shared within these pages will undoubtedly resonate with those aspiring to be leaders, experienced executives and change-makers in various industries. It certainly resonated with me.

As a reader, I resonated most with the authors' profound belief in the power of combining the heart and mind – the art and science – while steering the course of transformation. The authors elucidate that, like the inseparable strands of DNA, both aspects are critical for the success of any change initiative. My own experience of over three decades – first in Hindustan Unilever Limited and more recently as the Chief People and Transformation Officer at Unilever – wholly supports this notion. Over the years, I have had the opportunity to both witness and lead some large transformational initiatives.

Some were successful; others less so. Looking back at some of the less successful transformations, some themes emerge. Getting the balance between the head and heart wrong is right on top. In my experience, the lack of a compelling narrative – one that addresses the 'why?' and touches both hearts and minds of the organisation – alongside an obsessive focus on the 'what', or the transformation plan, without the willingness to listen and adapt the 'how', based on feedback, has been the undoing of many change initiatives.

There are other themes in the book that struck a chord. One is the importance of not seeing transformation as a sporadic endeavour but as cultivating a culture that constantly evolves and innovates. In a world where disruptive technologies and paradigm shifts have become the norm, the art of continuous transformation is essential for survival and success, particularly, the need to proactively envision the future during prosperous times.

And yet it's hard. That's why most transformations are undertaken when the business is in crisis, often struggling to stay relevant and fighting for survival. That makes a hard task even harder. Recent research from Bain & Company suggests that a mere 12 per cent of transformation initiatives achieve their intended objectives. The authors aptly point out that companies that fail to adapt and evolve are destined to perish in the long run. Consider this: the lifespan of companies listed today in the Standard & Poor's 500 is less than eighteen years – a stark contrast to the sixty-one-year lifespan seen in 1958 and a poignant reminder for contemporary leaders to embrace change wholeheartedly.

The book also introduces an intriguing concept: the 'adaptation quotient of future leaders', that is, the ability to interpret data and signals, even subtle ones, combined with the courage to challenge long-held industry assumptions, which lies at the core of creating transformational strategies. The authors' keen understanding of this balance between data-driven decision-making and intuition is a valuable lesson for any leader navigating uncharted waters.

In conclusion, I sincerely thank Gopal and Hrishi for sharing their profound wisdom, insights and experiences in this book. Their passion for transformative leadership is evident in every word. I am confident that this book will become an indispensable bedside companion for leaders at every stage of their journey, as a source of inspiration and guidance. I only wish this had been written a little earlier – I might have avoided some pitfalls in my own career!

Nitin Paranjpe
Chief People and Transformation Officer, Unilever PLC;
Chairman, Hindustan Unilever Limited

1

Heart plus Mind

The rise and fall of business dynasties always makes for educative reading. One of the descendants of the Vanderbilt family, Anderson Cooper, co-authored a fine book titled *Vanderbilt: The Rise and Fall of an American Dynasty* in late 2021.[1] A visit to The Breakers, the lavish Vanderbilt home in Rhode Island, reignited our interest in the fall of this dynasty.

As the founder of the dynasty, Cornelius 'Commodore' Vanderbilt, is reported to have told his son, 'Any fool can make a fortune; it takes a man of brains to hold it.' The founder had accumulated a US$100 million fortune at the time of his death (worth several billions of dollars in today's money) in 1877. As his son William Vanderbilt said some twenty-five years after his father's death, 'Inherited wealth is a real handicap to happiness … it has left me with nothing to hope for, with nothing definite to seek or strive for.'

Their fortune is believed to have been lost for two reasons: first, among the increasing numbers of the fourth generation onward, some of the family members became gamblers, while some others led an indolent lifestyle. Second – the reason more relevant to the theme of this book – freight through steamboats and railroads, the very basis on which the business had been founded, had begun to give way by the late 1920s, yielding fully to unexpected competition around the Second World War. Trucks, barges, airplanes and buses had taken over all the freight business. Some years later, there was no business left. The last-standing witness to the Vanderbilt history was The Breakers – standing as a mute testimony to what happens when business leaders fail to embrace the future and transform obsessively.

That is what this book aims to tackle.

It has been rewarding to write about organisational transformation as a live business subject. We first heard about a Chief Transformation Officer in India around 2000, when Tata Consultancy Services (TCS) appointed a full-time professional to do the job. At that time, S. Ramadorai was the Chief Executive Officer of TCS and he was undertaking a major growth initiative at the company with the assistance and guidance of a consulting academic. Not surprisingly, many of us were intrigued.

In the two decades that followed, we have watched other companies appoint a Chief Transformation Officer; for example, Tata Chemicals and the global consumer goods marketer Unilever. Such appointments suggest that transformation management has gradually become a top leadership issue. Therefore, it is entirely appropriate that the present Chief Transformation Officer, Unilever Global Leadership Executive, Nitin Paranjpe, has written the foreword to this book and the authors are truly delighted at his involvement. His appointment and his experiences are both highly relevant to the theme of this book. In his capacity as non-executive chairman of Hindustan Unilever Limited, Nitin delivered a speech at the Annual General Meeting in 2023 titled 'Transforming to Win in the New India', where he stated, 'Embracing change to remain future-fit enhances the company's capacity to adapt and lead change.'

Business transformation appeared in the management lexicon sometime during the last few decades, and the practice is still maturing. Business management is replete with new terminology that evolves periodically. Such new terminology can be classified into two compartments: the concept may either be brand new, for example, bottom-of-the-pyramid or frugal innovation; or a buzzword may emerge to represent an existing idea, but in a new form or shape, for example, innovation, cost control or technology.

A cursory survey of Ngram data for the period 1800–2000 indicates the following:
- 'Innovation' has been used as a word right from 1800. In the initial years, it had a negative connotation – to 'novate' – of being derisively attributed to an act of challenging existing well-established ideas, particularly in religion. After 1960, the use of the word 'innovation' escalated rapidly and consistently, right into modern times, and it is still rising.
- 'Cost control' and 'technology' have been longer-duration hardies, originating in the early 1900s and rising steadily after the 1980s.
- The expressions 'transformation management' and 'change management' were hardly in use from 1800 to 1960. Their usage wavered a bit in the 1960s, but after 1985, the use of the expression took off and now sits at an all-time peak.

Transformation management has now become a coveted vocation. Consulting companies sport a transformation practice much as they may have sported a marketing or supply chain practice earlier. Writing in the *Financial Times*,[2] John Gapper quotes a senior business leader as saying, 'I have never known so many CEOs stressed by their business models. I have never known a time of so many institutions thinking, "the glory days are behind us".' He concludes, 'When everything, from technology to supply chains and the environment, changes so fast, they grasp for solutions.'

The authors, as long-in-the-tooth managers with a combined experience of over a hundred years, were intrigued by this pattern. Such Ngram data from over two centuries suggests that much like in the world of botany and biology, in management ideas, practices and jargon too there is a birth–maturity–renewal cycle.

Nature, representing the world of biology and botany, teaches us three relevant lessons about transformative adaptation:
1. Adaptation is continual and not episodic.

2. Adaptation is obsessive. Constant alertness is essential for survival.
3. Responses are based on embracing or assessing the future rather than the past. As the adage goes, gazelles need not run faster than their predators, the leopards and cheetahs – a gazelle only needs to run faster than the next gazelle.

Traditional management teaching has focused on excellence. To promote functional excellence, the teaching has been focused on the parts: obsessiveness about customers in marketing; obsessiveness about efficiency in manufacturing; obsessiveness about clean balance sheets and profit/loss statements in finance, and so on.

Transformation management increasingly demands obsessiveness across every dimension of the enterprise simultaneously – the 'what to do' (strategy) as well as the 'who will get it done' (people). The challenge is not about transformation management, but rather about transformation leadership.

Many practitioners assume that if you know what to do, the how to do it will fall into place. That is why the strategy function is thought to be superior, and tends to attract the brighter talent from MBA classes. To emphasise the holistic approach we have adopted in this book, we have placed the 'how to' portion ahead of the 'what to' portion.

Obsessive leadership in business transformation is about leading by 'heart plus mind'. The most appropriate way for us to test this hypothesis was, of course, to do so against the century of joint corporate experience that was embedded in our minds.

Our Experiences

We began our professional careers at about the same time, in the same company. We shared dissimilar journeys along the network of pathways for thirty years. During the last twenty years of our professional lives our paths and experiences diverged.

When we began our careers in HLL (then Hindustan Lever), we found a company that was convulsing with an 'earthquake' called 'sales reorganisation'. Just before we joined, the legendary chairman of HLL Prakash Tandon had led this sales reorganisation effort with the goal of transforming the company. At the core of the reorganisation was the objective to combine three sales forces into two, with the strategic intent of saving costs and improving the efficiency of delivering to market. We will describe what that reorganisation effort was about later in the book. Rather, we will focus on the *effect* that the transformation had on our young and still-maturing managerial minds.

We found the company in turmoil. We could not understand what we had got into because the external perception of HLL was that it was a steady, ethical and well-run company – which, of course, it was, even though it was temporarily reeling from a sales reorganisation. The sales force was deeply upset – everyone for his or her own reasons – and the middle and senior managements were divided in their opinions. The top team was insistent that the idea was good and that managers should focus on executing the good idea. Throughout our internship, we made our personal observations and formed our own views, which we naturally kept confined to our private chatter.

As it so happened, Prakash Tandon retired soon after and Vasant Rajadhyaksha succeeded him as Chairman. The new top team took a few months to reverse the reorganisation. It was not quite to status quo ante, but a modified version of the previous order.

During the following years, the Indian labour market increased in turbulence due to many factors unconnected with this reorganisation. The massive internal churn and rechurn within HLL affected its employees, distributors and managers. It aggravated a developing unrest into an acute industrial relations challenge, which was tackled by top leadership right through the 1970s – that story is for later.

During the sales reorganisation, we both sensed that to make change or transformation, a leader needs an intellectually appealing change that can naturally win over the minds of the affected people. Such change or transformation must also be accompanied by appealing propositions that would win over their hearts.

'Heart plus mind' was our idiosyncratic lesson. No great rocket science.

Our naïve hypothesis was that while the sales reorganisation effort held indisputable appeal to the minds of the people, it may have slipped up on appealing to their hearts. We carried our simplistic ideas within our minds as we embarked on our respective career paths over the next twenty years.

By the early 1980s, both of us were in senior positions. Around this time, another reorganisation became imminent. This time, however, we both would have the opportunity to plan, design and implement the change. Our days of armchair criticism and commentary were about to end. When the top leadership nominated a team to conceive and implement this reorganisation, we both were enlisted. Hrishi and I were joined by an affable colleague of ours, Dicky Saldanha.

At that time, as a seasoned brand aficionado, Hrishi was heading marketing in the branded tea business of Lipton India, an associate but separate firm. Dicky came from the manufacturing stream of HLL – literally a blue-eyed manager with an up-and-coming career, and humorous to boot. Gopal was heading the oils, fats, dairy and animal feeds business of HLL.

Through an inter-company transfer of businesses, the boards had decided to spin off the oils, fats, animal feeds and dairy businesses of HLL into Lipton India. This would enable Lipton India to cease operating as a single business (tea) and diversify the company into the oils, fats, animal feeds and dairy businesses as well, apart from the traditional tea business.

The three of us had diverse backgrounds – brand marketing, manufacturing, commodities management – but we shared the common Unilever culture. We had fiercely different points of view, but we were open in our discussions and attempts to resolve our differences. This process was greatly enabled by at least two factors. First, we were all about the same age and with similar years of professional experience. Second, Dicky had a mirthful mannerism, converting every knotty issue into a light joke, which immediately defused the tension amongst ourselves or with our bosses.

In discharging our remit, we were influenced by the logical and the emotional. Thus, instead of dreaming up dazzling and revolutionary solutions to issues, we chose the less risky method of favouring plausible and evolutionary solutions. We recommended a first and second step, with the proviso that a clearer end-state might take shape only over three or four years. An integral part of our recommendation was to allow time for four important aspects – talk time, soak time, mellowing time and response time among the affected people.

Even though we say so ourselves, we think it worked alright; the solutions were not greatly elegant, but fit the purpose.

Thereafter, our careers diverged again, though in parallel and satisfying ways. This book is not about that HLL–Lipton India reorganisation, hence the details of the challenges and the solutions have deliberately been scant. We would like to comment more on what we learned about organisational transformation from that experience: heart plus mind!

Gopal went on to become the chairman of a Unilever overseas subsidiary, Unilever Arabia, where he was tasked with merging eleven joint ventures (JVs) across the Gulf Cooperation Council nations into a well-knit, autonomous corporation. It was yet another blockbuster transformation experience, though it came so soon after the previous one.

The lesson was reiterated: heart plus mind.

Parallelly, the decade-old, reorganised Lipton India was also merged into another associate company, Brooke Bond India.

Just as we thought that the transformation was complete, yet another five years later, the merged Brooke Bond Lipton India was merged into Hindustan Lever. Reorganisations and transformations were increasing in complexity and in frequency.

In fact, when Gopal assumed office in 1995, as the CEO of Brooke Bond Lipton India (BBLIL for short), there were eight acquired companies to be merged into an integrated whole. Transformation no longer seemed like an occasional event – it now seemed like an omnipresent part of every business leader's agenda!

After serving for thirty-one years, during Gopal's tenure as Hindustan Lever's vice chairman, he met Ratan Tata, the eponymous chairman of the holding company of the Tata Group, Tata Sons Limited. Ratan Tata explained a role he had in mind for someone who would work with him on the transformation of the century-old Tata Group. By this time, Gopal had started to view transformation as a key role of business leaders; so, he switched from his transformation-preoccupied role at Hindustan Lever to Tata Sons. What an exciting ride that was!

Ratan Tata had already designed a blueprint for the transformation of the group. Along with a few other senior members, Gopal was to function as a part of the top team. He was thus afforded a ringside seat, getting to participate both as a player and as an observer in the transformation journey of Tata.

Ratan Tata had architected this plan a few years earlier, when he assumed chairmanship and was faced with the challenges of economic liberalisation in the wake of the 1991 reforms; he was compelled to respond. While Gopal was at Unilever, he had had the chance to see how HLL responded to liberalisation around the same time as well, so he was in a unique position to compare, contrast and learn.

His experience was so compelling that we have included a write-up on this aspect later in the book. The overarching lesson was that both leaders, Susim Datta at HLL and Ratan Tata at Tata, developed a rigorous analytical strategy to respond to the reforms, but both used a significantly intuitive, human approach to execution.

Once again, heart plus mind.

Hrishi's formative years were spent in sales in the eastern and southern regions of India, and in managing brands like Surf and Fair & Lovely. He learnt to be outward-looking, bringing those learnings and observations into the business as well. He rose through the ranks at HLL, Brooke Bond and Lipton, gathering insights into the washing products, personal care, skincare and beverages markets. It was at Lipton that he engaged in a serious strategy play to turn around the large but sick domestic tea business.

Back in HLL as Marketing and Sales Director, he led the strategy and implementation of curtailing the prospects of a major international competitor entering India and, in the process, brought much-needed expansion and growth to the business portfolio. He spent the subsequent years in Brazil, where he integrated a major acquisition, and in the Unilever headquarters (HQ) in the Netherlands, where he was Senior Vice President – Worldwide of the newly formed health and wellness category. This was the period when he observed first-hand many societies and businesses around the world, learning what makes them similar, and what makes them different, and most important, what makes them successful.

Primarily engaged in strategy work, he slowly got interested in academic work in the area as well. Dr C.K. Prahalad, the renowned management guru, Hrishi and John Ripley, a Unilever colleague, worked together on Project Foresight to find new opportunities for Unilever in the new millennium.

CK became an intellectual partner, mentor and close friend in the time he and Hrishi taught at the University of Michigan, Ann Arbor, and published some papers together. Hrishi was also deeply influenced by Michael Porter and Clayton Christensen of Harvard, Jim Collins and Jerry Porras of Stanford, A.G. Lafley of Procter and Gamble (P&G), Roger Martin of Rotman School, Steve Jobs of Apple, John Kotter of Harvard, and W. Chan Kim and Renee Mauborgne of INSEAD, to name a few, from whose thoughts and ideas he liberally borrowed, to adapt and use in his own teaching, writings and consulting work.

National Experiences

Growing up in a newly independent India, we have also witnessed change and transformation in matters concerning the nation. Just as both our careers were born in HLL's sales reorganisation, we ourselves were born amid the ravages of a newly partitioned India. Initially, we were too young to comprehend and reflect on the major developments. As we grew up, the revolutionary change unleashed by the quixotic, maybe impetuous, acts of imperialism dawned on us – like inviting an Englishman, a first-time visitor to India, to partition the country by the act of drawing a line with his pencil across the map; or announcing a British withdrawal date just two months before 15 August 1947, that too without giving any notice to the Indian political leaders who had been spearheading the national movement of independence for years! However, these were post facto lessons for us.

We were, however, more aware when Hindi was announced as the sole national language in the early 1950s in an India whose people spoke about thirty major languages and 800 dialects. There was mayhem when the southern Dravidian states protested violently. The then government retracted the law and suggested a solution – certain concurrent languages for fifteen years. That proviso has now continued for seventy-five years, much to the irritation of Hindi lobbyists, but serving as a soothing balm to the non-Hindi-speaking states.

Not orchestrated by the political class, an emerging Bollywood, with its oblique artistic and commercial interests and its vast community of actors, musicians, filmmakers and poets, unleashed Hindi film entertainment onto the Indian people, several of whom sought inexpensive respite from their Dickensian existences in the years after Independence. Through films, Hindi gradually permeated the pockets of resistance. We have memories of watching the Hindi blockbuster *Sampoorna Ramayana* on television in Chikmagalur, Karnataka, and *Kaun Banega Crorepati* in Kumbakonam, Tamil Nadu.

Another transformation management episode that we grew up witnessing was the state response to family planning. During the 1950s, it became a national imperative to reduce the replacement rate of population to control population growth. By the time we began our careers in the late 1960s, private sector companies like HLL and some others had been enlisted by the government to popularise and distribute a male protection device, called Nirodh. We were both in our early twenties, slim with jet-black hair, not yet concerned with matters of sex and protection, and certainly incapable of communicating about these openly with strangers. Both of us were frustrated and amused by our experience of introducing the product into retail trade, explaining what exactly it was and how it was to be used.

In those days, the Directorate of Audio-Visual Publicity (DAVP), a government agency, ran a family planning campaign in newspapers and films. It depicted a young, newly married couple in all their adornments, who were exhorted by the advertising copy or voiceovers to avoid having a baby for at least five years. The messaging was clear, yet the campaign failed miserably.

Upon investigating the reasons for this, it emerged that in the India of those days – perhaps even now, though to a lesser extent – young married women were not allowed the choice to decide whether or not they wanted to bear a child and would be pressurised by their families much before completing five years of marriage.

Sensibly, the DAVP changed their approach to show a young couple with one child in arms, and the appeal was now changed to avoiding having a second child for five years. This sensitivity, along with several other innovations and communications, worked.

Nowadays India's birth rate is quite close to the replacement rate. This is a remarkable success story, not told as often, drowned out by the din of contemporary politics. No other society among emerging nations has achieved this outcome peaceably, though the time taken by India was longer, because it was done in an 'evolutionary' manner rather than a revolutionary manner. Quite in line with the principle of 'Heart plus Mind'.

Just as the Ngram data alluded to in the beginning, we have experienced that change and transformation management have both become 'sitting members' of the agenda of top leaders. Their importance seems to match that of competing imperatives like digitisation, planet and people, conscious capitalism, and so on. This is what triggered the idea of a book that would speak to both the 'art' and 'science' aspects of transformation.

The Art and Science of Transformation

After his retirement from Unilever, Hrishi took on an academic and consulting avatar. He taught at the University of Michigan alongside the fabled Professor C.K. Prahalad. He honed his philosophy of strategy, its importance and the pros and cons of various disciplined approaches.

After Gopal's retirement from Tata, he began to write a monthly column in The *New Indian Express* on the soft aspects of transformation management. Quite by accident, therefore, the authors found that they possessed two matching gloves, one right and one left, both having equal importance for the subject we had encountered together and individually during our respective careers. A subsequent conversation between two old friends resulted in the creation of this book.

We must confess that we were influenced by the profiles of some top professionals in their field, successful people who synthesised their sense of rationality and science with their sense of art and emotion. Dr Homi Bhabha was legendary not only for his scientific prowess but also for his passion for music. J.R.D. Tata was not only a great 'leader of business leaders', he was also a humanistic individual who spoke about the need for 'affectionate leaders'. Mumbai's famed physician, Dr Farrokh Udwadia, spoke of the equal importance of 'science and art' in healing. In one interview, he worried about the increasing role of technology and machines in diagnosis and treatment among new doctors, somewhat ignoring the warmth of personal connection with the patient and 'bedside manners'.

Our own observations and experiences, buttressed by the profiles of professionals outside the field of management, have caused us to divide this book into two parts. The authors worked together on the whole book and accept joint ownership for both parts, though for reasons of practicality and interest, each part has been written by one or the other author.

The first part dwells on the art – the soft and the behavioural aspects of transformation management. The second part dwells on science – the analytical and intellectual aspects of transformation management. Put together in a single book, these aspects make up the whole of our expertise on transformation management. Without making too tall a claim, we feel that such a practical exposition is not as readily available to management practitioners in India as it ought to be. Our backgrounds enabled us to fuse together learnings from Indian as well as international organisations to support our arguments and experiences.

Many managers spend a lot of their time and energy correcting mistakes from the past. They become reactive to the actions of competitors and the regulatory environment and often find that their own companies are in a major crisis, if they are not themselves in an existential one. Cost-cutting, layoffs and organisational restructuring then become the order of the day.

Many of these actions are essential and required. But they come as a result of managers clinging to the past and, therefore, seldom result in real, long-term gains. Looking ahead during good times, figuring out the next practice and getting ahead of everyone else through a combined heart-and-mind approach may indeed be the durable benefit of a transformation mindset.

Fifty years ago, transformation and reorganisation were widely regarded as one-time, important events. Increasingly, it is seen as a continuous process. We refer to this as 'continuous transformation'.

We recall the story about Cummins Engine Company, the world's most successful diesel engine company, headquartered in Columbus, Indiana, in the United States. The company was led by a long-serving CEO and Chairman called J. Irwin Miller for over five decades. The company's business sat squarely in a highly capital-intensive industry, which was, additionally, highly cyclical. Perhaps it was these economic fundamentals that fostered the change-oriented culture that is the hallmark of Cummins. 'Obsolete your own products' was an important maxim attributed to Irwin Miller. After Miller retired, he was succeeded by Henry Schacht as Chairman and CEO.

Henry Schacht attributed the company's long-term success to its willing embrace of change in these powerful words:[3]

> Change is a way of life. An industrial company should seize upon change as opportunity. It should look forward to change; it should thrive on change; but, most of all, it should create and force change rather than react to change created by others.
>
> Change is healthy. Creating and forcing change is the prime job of any management, no matter what the institution or group, no matter what the location.

This exemplary message would appeal to a leader's rational mind. However, the heart's yearning for stability and calm is pitched against this call for change. It is in this maelstrom that organisations get sucked in, fighting for survival and growth.

No book can expound any last word on transformation management, which is an increasingly frequent preoccupation of company leaders. There is no such thing as a last word on any subject, anyway, in a highly dynamic world that is constantly changing.

As authors, we sincerely hope that by writing this book, we are able to make a modest contribution to thought leadership and the vital practice of business transformation.

Part 1

The Soft Aspects of Transformation

R. Gopalakrishnan

2

Software

Transformation as Art

The difference between transactional management and transformational leadership is about how change is managed. Is holistic transformation leadership another jawbreaker of mumbo-jumbo? Not in the context of this book. It is akin to a holistic life.

With the deep impact of technology on productivity and ways of working, executives appropriately rely on rationality in change management – perhaps to a fault. As machine learning (ML) and artificial intelligence (AI) emerge, this trend of left-brained-ness has a high probability of gathering pace. Rational thinking is a crucial skill for operational managers, for whom efficiency and delivery of results are key. MBA students, in fact, are educated in transactional knowledge. During the first half of their careers, young executives are rightly rewarded by their employers for displaying rationality.

Then their careers arrive at a crossroads. One is a straight path, which continues to demand dominantly rational approaches. The other path appears more uncertain, like a steep, winding gradient, like the path encountered by a mountain or rock climber. This second path demands intuitive skills because the straight and rational path has ended – it is important to note here that an empathetic approach is not an alternative to a rational approach, but rather an adjunct.

In transactional management, the manager responds to issues keeping a near-term horizon in mind, persuading people to follow action plans. For example, a decision about the production, sales or profit target in the next quarter, or a no-go decision in the penultimate stages of a new product launch by a certain date.

Transformational leadership, on the other hand, requires adaptive responses, keeping in view individuals and social systems. In this mode, followers feel empowered and engaged; they feel a sense of self-identity and take ownership of their results. For example, should the company execute a good plan that will create considerable opposition within? If yes, how can the opposition to the plan be mitigated? What effort is required to do so?

This is the big difference. But the two approaches also overlap. They deploy rationality and intuition in different proportions: transactional management requires dominant rational skills, while transformational leadership requires dominant intuitive skills.

Both skill sets are relevant.

A holistic leadership approach is akin to a systems approach: the impact of one decision on every other part of the moving system is contemplated in advance. Rather than describing the differences, I shall illustrate through the exceptional and noteworthy example of corporate rationalisation in Tata Steel (TISCO) in the early 1990s, when Dr Jamshed Irani led the company. I do not intend to analyse or comment on every aspect of the rather massive transformation, but to merely illustrate what a 'holistic' approach looks like.

TISCO has had a long history of harmonious and trusting industrial relations. In the late 1980s, Dr Irani recalls a conversation with J.R.D. Tata outside Jamshedpur Steel Works. JRD bemoaned the fact that the chief engineer, Mr Firoze Tarapore, had submitted as many modernisations for the company as the years in his life. But from where was TISCO to get the funds? Irani doggedly responded that unless TISCO was modernised urgently, leaders would soon be standing at the factory gate, selling tickets to visit a steel museum. It was a grim but forthright assessment of the future.

Then the environment changed. Liberalisation was announced by the government. It was an 'aha!' moment for Dr Jamshed Irani and his leadership team. Very quickly, TISCO's efficiency was benchmarked by comparing it with top global companies. A system of Total Business Excellence was adopted to rapidly improve wherever TISCO was lagging. The old plans were updated with contemporary ideas of technology and productivity, thus producing a fresh modernisation plan. Huge funds were required; so funding ideas were developed accordingly. In a sense, these were all in the realm of the rational – technology, funding, productivity, sustainability and so on.

There was a deep understanding that implementing these ideas was going to be a long game, stretching across years, maybe a decade. Taking a systems approach, the leadership realised that their grandiose plans required a fundamental change of mindset to successfully rationalise the manpower from 80,000 to 40,000; simultaneously, the employee profile had to transform to younger, differently skilled manpower.

The fact is that an intimate cause-and-effect relationship exists between technically sound ideas on the one hand, and individuals and social systems on the other. TISCO would have to adapt to unprecedented manpower reduction in Jamshedpur – perhaps even unparalleled anywhere in any Indian company at that time – after halving the manpower in what was essentially a company township!

A carefully thought-out set of schemes was devised by operational and human resource (HR) leaders to implement this manpower rationalisation. The CEO, leadership team and the board chairman spent hours in discussions. The leadership did not regard it as a headcount reduction but rather as an unavoidable surgery on the delicate body of the company.

This led to thinking about the employees with great empathy. How could the company achieve the result with the least pain, considering pain and bleeding could not be avoided?

Employees were met in small groups and large groups; in the factory and in their community setting. Questions were answered with empathy, but also with firmness. For example, at one town-hall meeting, a senior employee questioned Dr Irani, 'This company has a commitment to employ one son of each family, a practice that has existed for several decades. What happens to that?'

Irani responded, 'I understand your anguish; please appreciate that the issue at hand is not about employment for your son, it is about your own employment!'

A scheme was devised whereby employees above a certain age and term of service would receive the full basic salary right up to their retirement age. Younger employees were given a lump sum and guided towards entrepreneurship. Counsellors were engaged to speak to distressed families, sparing no effort to do the surgery with the finest bedside manners.

Finally, TISCO did modernise technologically; its productivity rivalled the best in the world within a few years, as evidenced by a report of World Steel Dynamics, a global steel body of manufacturers. In addition, the company rationalised manpower from 80,000 to 40,000. No leader felt good about this surgery, but the patient, namely, the company, was saved.

The example illustrates the distinction between transformational leadership and transactional management.

A Collective Legend about the Future

In my native Tamil language, a single letter like 'ka' represents four letters of Sanskrit, 'ka', 'kha', 'ga', 'gha'. The pronunciation of the letter in a word is determined by the letters that precede and follow it. 'Carton' and 'Garden' are written the same way in Tamil, but what precedes and follows a letter determine the word's meaning and pronunciation. I quote this linguistic tendency as a metaphor for inclusiveness in society – what is adjacent, what precedes and what follows is important to fully appreciate a person. In organisational transformations also, what precedes and what follows a change add meaning to the proposed decision or action.

Transformations are necessarily painful, as the reader would also have experienced in their own lives and so can easily imagine. An important reason for pain is the lack of a collective legend about the future. A collective legend is a distinctive story about the future that has been developed by people on an inclusive basis, by involving the employees.

A collective legend is an intense and painfully democratic process, full of compromises and adjustments. Think about the transition years of India's independence – how the Constituent Assembly developed the Indian Constitution, or how the Nehru–Mahalanobis model explained planning to the people of India. Inclusiveness means that the *context* that a person is placed in is as important as its *implication* for the person.

Just by way of illustration, Hershey's Chocolate Company was and is a storied Pennsylvania-based company, which has existed for over a century. Much like Jamshedpur, the founder's stamp – the communitarian orientation of Milton Hershey – was incorporated into the company's policies and practices over a hundred years. And then something odd occurred in the 1990s, by which time financial investors were putting great pressure on company leaders to keep on increasing growth and profits.

With a change in management, the new CEO designed a cost reduction programme to improve the profitability of the company. In a dramatic move, he shut down three plants. He asked the long-serving Hershey employees to pay a higher price for their families' medical expenses. The ideas may have been sound from a rational point of view, but the soft side of communication and building a collective legend about the future was lost for the employees. They took to the streets of the company township to protest against and block the proposed changes.

Democracy and authoritarianism are not natural companions. In long-surviving organisations, there is likely to be a collective and valuable memory about the past; but as we move from the present to the future, divergent views are likely to emerge. We see this in companies, societies and nations.

At a national and society level, the divergent views about the present and the future manifest as ethnic or religious narcissism. A particular religious or ethnic group is proclaimed to be original, while the remaining are portrayed as 'others'. Leaders hark back to a glorious past and seek to revive the mythical 'good old days'. Integrating the people of a diverse nation or company is not easy.

In my own small way, I had two experiences during the 1990s: one in Jeddah, integrating eleven JVs in the Middle East into a cohesive Unilever overseas subsidiary called Unilever Arabia. A few years later again – this time in India – I was entrusted with integrating eight companies, which were merged to form Brooke Bond Lipton India Limited. I shall describe the lessons that I learnt in a later part of this book.

Old Dying but New Yet Unborn

The elephant in the room is that the old has not been fully discarded and the new is not quite established. Thanks to hindsight, I have an important lesson to offer in the challenges of developing a collective legend. The leadership speaks with its eye on the future, while the employees and associates receive its messages with their eyes on the past. Transformation represents the interregnum when the individual's sense of vulnerability increases and when multiple emotions – anxiety, anger, disillusionment – may coalesce into an unhealthy apathy to act in line with what is required by the company.

In this maelstrom of emotions and vulnerability, you need leaders who are intellectual nomads. An intellectual nomad is one who approaches the transformation challenge with an empathetic open mind, a determination to listen, and a will to relearn old truths. Without such an approach, the pain of transformation can get heightened.

In the transition between the old and the new, a planned or inadvertent 'othering' develops between the 'real' and the 'pretenders'. Every individual wants to be heard; that is a basic human want. Leaders must invest in formal and informal ways to listen; above all, they must be seen as listening, otherwise disillusion grows and trust declines among employees. This is understandable, because with the loss of our voice, a part of us gets lost. This can be minimised when leaders reach out and listen, especially to the weakest members in the ecosystem.

In the 1990s, South Africa was transforming from an apartheid-ridden society to a 'rainbow nation'. Nelson Mandela wanted to show support for South Africa in the World Cup Rugby finals at Johannesburg in 1995. Because the Springboks team was historically white, his advisers dissuaded him from attending. Mandela did the opposite, showing up at the event wearing the Springboks jersey and cheering for the national team. He demonstrated that othering hinders transformation.

When Gandhiji wished to emotionally connect with the common Indian, he shed Western attire for the loincloth, travelled in third class by train and learned how to use the spinning wheel. By showing empathy, he managed to touch millions of Indians with his ideal of *ahimsa*. He lived by his advice to others, 'Be the change you want to see in the world.'

When M.G. Ramachandran proposed expanding the Kamaraj-planned midday meal scheme to schools in Tamil Nadu in the late 1970s – a revolutionary move for the times – he faced bureaucratic resistance on account of budgets. It is reported that he asked his officers in an emotional tone, '*Pasi na ennendu ungallukku theriyuma? Nan thaanga midiyada pasi therinjirken* (Have you experienced real hunger? I have experienced unbearable hunger).'[1] That did it. Tamil Nadu introduced the expanded scheme and improved the lives of the people greatly in the fifty years that followed this move.

When evaluating the implementation of the Amul model (in which surplus skimmed milk and butter fat would be imported and recombined to make milk when farmers got less milk from their herd), Lal Bahadur Shastri spent time (including one night incognito) with dairy farmers to personally understand the implications of the Amul experiment started by Dr V. Kurien. Indeed, Dr Kurien prided himself to be an employee of the farmers despite his 'otherness' as a Kerala Christian and a foreign-trained engineer.

Companies, and indeed the nation, seek rapid and sustainable growth to alleviate poverty and shed old-fashioned beliefs. Leaders need to do more to develop a collective legend and demonstrate empathy for the needs of their people.

My Experience at Unilever Arabia

I would like to share my personal experiences of organisational transformation in Unilever Arabia between 1990 and 1994 (of integrating eleven JVs) and in BBLIL between 1994 and 1998 (of integrating eight acquisitions). I request that readers may read these within the context of this book.

In the interest of brevity, I propose to view the experience through a conceptual rather than an operational lens. The learnings may appear like motherhood statements. In my defence, I affirm that the self-evident lessons are the ones that leaders tend to forget during transformation management. It is useful to learn and practise the skills of an anthropologist, namely, to observe, listen, record and reflect, all without judgement!

I recall that I had memorised a mantra to guide my daily routines during this phase of my career, the mnemonic for which was 'SCULPT', standing for Socialisation, Communication,

Understanding, Learning, Patience, Trust. This was a learning outcome of a programme that I had attended at INSEAD, Fontainebleau, about how to get the best out of a diverse workforce. There are five lessons to embellish the SCULPT mnemonic.

In most transformations, the bottleneck, or 'crux', as it is called,[2] is adaptiveness of the team. In summary, the true value of an HR professional as a key ally is palpable during transformations.

Lesson 1: Recruit early and ally with the HR chief
Colin Davie, a high-performing employee in Unilever, was my first recruit. He became the HR chief at Unilever Arabia. R.R. Nair, an accomplished professional, had been the HR chief at BBLIL at the time of my joining. I had deep conversations with both the HR chiefs and I was able to appreciate the incredible value of their words. Meetings with them sometimes took precedence over those with other colleagues, though this was quite the opposite of what CEOs generally do, giving higher priority to marketing, operations and finance heads. I must emphasise here that while operational functions possess a greater natural gravitas, the CEO must accord special focus to the HR function while implementing a transformation.

Lesson 2: Interact with the least powerful people in the ecosystem
I used to travel to distant and less-visited operations to connect with factory workers and salespeople. It was strenuous but worthwhile going to Gisan, Tabuk and Gassim in Saudi Arabia, and Tundla, Kanhan, Ghatkesar and Etah in India, during my time at BBLIL.

I learnt about the deep-rooted suspicions between managers from Lipton India and employees of Brooke Bond, arising out of eighty years of being market competitors. In Arabia, the Lipton teabag business earned so much of the Unilever

Arabia's cash flows that its people silently disapproved of the company's move to reinvest that cash in 'the dud business of detergents'! Reaching out and listening carefully for any subtle messages circulating among the workers proved greatly beneficial for me in facilitating organisational transformation as a leader.

Lesson 3: Formalise mechanisms for employee feedback
While informal methods of listening by leadership are important, they are not a substitute for formal channels. At BBLIL, HR chief R.R. Nair began an extended series at the company's training centre, branding it as 'Confluence Series'. Almost twenty-five sessions were held, each hosting thirty to forty managers for an evening. Nair and I attended every session, thus connecting with about 1,000 company executives. I learnt that merging balance sheets is easier than aligning mindsets.

In Arabia, whenever I travelled, Colin Davie invariably arranged a lunch or formal meeting with the local managers in Bahrain, Kuwait, Dubai, Riyadh and elsewhere. For me, these sessions were crucial. I had to train myself to listen to people without judging them, which is not very easy to do in a hierarchical organisation.

Lesson 4: Use the burning platform to stimulate change
One must maintain a delicate balance between imparting a sense of urgency for change and avoiding a sense of doom or desperation among the executives. There was a continuous tussle between the advocates of continuity and the advocates of change. Both consultation with the HR chief and early experimentation proved immensely valuable. I was passionately invested in receiving feedback from my HR chiefs after every communication session. I sought feedback to the point of appearing vulnerable to my HR chief – but it is important to remember that the HR chief is the only professional to

whom the CEO can express personal vulnerability without creating organisation-wide doubts about the confidence of the leadership. Luckily, my colleagues were frank about how the session could have been more effective, and so we could improve.

Unilever Arabia was set up just after Saddam Hussein's invasion of Kuwait, a war that mercifully concluded within three months. Times were stressful enough for Unilever managers to consider expatriation from the territory. At BBLIL, on the other hand, the Narasimha Rao–Manmohan Singh government had introduced liberalisation. The measures threw up issues of cost benchmarking and competitiveness. The personal trauma of this on long-standing managers was intense. Their self-image was one of established competence; to look into the mirror and accept their glaring deficiencies was a big challenge.

Lesson 5: Communicate constantly, but both ways
I learned that a CEO should never tire of explaining the same thing repeatedly without showing irritation or impatience. This is not easy for a CEO, who is usually also perennially short on time. Patience and understanding are essential. My perception at that time was that the advice of both my HR chiefs acted like soft brakes on a speeding automobile, hampering my leadership. Both HR chiefs advised me on my deficiencies in leading the company effort, reminding me gently of a Korean proverb that it is precisely when you want to speed up that often you must slow down.

I must add that the challenge of leading the transformation was not just mine; it was the shared effort of a highly engaged and committed corporate leadership team.

Role of Luck

How important is luck in achieving transformation goals? Luck is a controversial subject. Some believe that relying on luck makes people easy-going. Others believe that luck is an indisputable part of reality. But change agents cannot rely on luck to deliver results – one must do one's very best, come what may. However, it is also important for the leadership to accept the reality that luck may play a negative or positive role in the result of the effort.

In the film *A Streetcar Named Desire*, Stanley Kowalski (Marlon Brando) said, 'You know what luck is? Luck is believing that you are lucky, that's all.' Was he right?

Psychologists have identified four moods produced by luck. If we have bad luck, we feel that we had no control over that event. If we have good luck, we believe that our actions had a lot to do with the result. If someone else has good luck, we feel jealous. We may feel a mean sense of joy, what the Germans call *schadenfreude*. The absence of causality in matters concerning luck is clear to the discerning.

The greatest challenge that leaders face – in companies, organisations or governments – is how to adapt to a rapidly changing environment. Before the 1980s, leaders were required to possess high intelligence (intelligence quotient or IQ); then came the era of empathy (emotional quotient or EQ), but of late, there seems to be a tendency towards their adaptability quotient (AQ). For leaders of tomorrow, possessing high IQ, EQ and AQ is surely the biggest challenge of leadership. I have touched upon the pitfalls to be avoided, people strengths that should be leveraged and illustrated the essential principles, through the examples of Hindustan Unilever and TISCO responding to the challenges posed by liberalisation.

Did the transformation efforts at Unilever, Tata or any other comparable organisation succeed purely because of their strategies? For sure, their results were indeed influenced by their plans and actions. But if someone else followed the same actions, can success be assured? The answer is no. Transformation programmes do not follow the laws of physics; therefore, there is no cause–effect relationship between actions and outcomes. In the words of Sir Isaac Newton, 'I can calculate the motions of heavenly bodies, but I cannot understand the madness of men.'

In great companies, continuous adaptation over decades has produced the dramatic and compounded effect of adaptability. We should not underestimate the benefits of compounding over a long period of time. Billionaire Warren Buffett created his wealth by investing cleverly over a long period of time – most of his wealth accumulated due to the time factor, not the cleverness factor.

Independent India has executed multiple transformation programmes. These have been reasonably successful. Examples of these include its constitutional democratic system of governance, five-year plans, population control programmes, the Green Revolution and the White Revolution. While all these initiatives are imperfect in their own ways, they have endured over decades and shown positive signs of maintaining sustainable success in the future.

People have their own beliefs on the debate between talent and luck. A study showed that the most talented individuals are not necessarily the most successful. Individuals with a 'median' level of talent who were favoured by luck tended to experience higher success. A paper by Cornell University suggested that while western culture places a high value on effort, talent and risk-taking, a large proportion of success can also be attributed to luck and random chance.[3]

An article titled 'Are "Great" Companies Just Lucky?'[4] argued that high-performing companies owe their success to luck, not to smart practices. The analytics-oriented consulting firm McKinsey, however, asserts that there are seven principles for achieving transformational growth (McKinsey Insights, 22 April 2021) luck notwithstanding.[5]

There is a bewildering array of conclusions and hypotheses. That is why managers should reflect on the following questions: What is luck? Is there a difference between 'earned' luck and 'unearned' luck? Does luck play a role in achieving success? How should a change-maker think about luck?

In my book titled *Six Lenses*,[6] I have devoted a whole chapter to the subject of luck. A reader from Goa criticised me for doing so, considering my credentials as 'an educated and enlightened student of physics, engineering and management'. In short, my learning has been: do your darndest best at things that you can control or influence. Thereafter, do not despair over how things may turn out.

Liberalisation and Hindustan Lever

HLL was a legacy business enjoying over a century of existence, through decades of colonialism, socialism, liberalisation and nationalism. It is one of the foremost Indian multinational companies. In this section, I will illustrate the transformational efforts of HLL by recounting its responses to the cataclysmic challenges presented by liberalisation in 1991. Since enough time has elapsed, this bit can be treated as instructive. I will attempt to address the following three questions:

(i) What went on inside the companies as liberalisation unfolded?
(ii) What new degrees of freedom did the companies obtain from liberalisation?
(iii) What were their dilemmas and how did they resolve them?

In 1990 the newly appointed Chairman, Susim Datta, had inherited a strong company, despite the licence-permit raj. The vexatious issue of 51 per cent foreign equity for Unilever under the Foreign Exchange Regulation Act (FERA) had lasted through the 1970s and 1980s. It got resolved through the strenuous efforts of the two previous chairmen after a decade-long legal battle. Being a FERA company, HLL had not been allowed to increase production or source its products from third parties.

Therefore, the company could not respond effectively to the detergent market share threat posed by Nirma, since the early 1970s.

HLL had grabbed at the invitation of the Punjab government to buy into the equity of an ailing government-owned detergent company, Stepan Chemicals. Being outside the ambit of FERA, Stepan Chemicals was permitted to source products from third parties. What a circuitous route to enhance production capacity! To adapt to FERA, HLL entered the chemicals and exports businesses, both of which had stabilised reasonably. But if there was to be liberalisation, these just-stabilised businesses would have to face fresh challenges.

From the early 1980s, the winds of change had begun wafting through government corridors. These winds did not develop into a gale because of political impediments. In 1990, it became obvious to Susim Datta that dramatic change was around the corner, though nobody knew what the change would look like and how dramatic it would be. For many decades, international business leaders had advocated for a liberal, free and consumer-driven market as a panacea for national development. This became a real possibility in May 1991, when Prime Minister P.V. Narasimha Rao (industry portfolio), Dr Manmohan Singh (finance portfolio) and P. Chidambaram (commerce portfolio) embarked on liberalising industry and trade. HLL was psychologically prepared for big change, however, there was no detailed company plan because the contours of the change were still unknown.

In the early days of liberalisation, the company engaged the services of Professor Sumantra Ghoshal of the London Business School to work with the leadership team. HLL developed alternative scenarios with an aggressive vision: to double sales every four years and double profits after tax every three years. This was akin to a pilot targeting to break the sound barrier with no prior experience of a sonic boom – the pace of change would increase to a level which nobody had any experience of working at before.

The six factories that had existed since the 1960s were sold or closed over time due to labour issues, product obsolescence or uncompetitive cost structures. Now HLL could set up new capacities without enduring the painful process of applying for industrial licences. Before 1991, HLL had already built a couple of new factories, thanks to a government policy for furthering industrially backward areas of the country. These were modern factories with new work practices. Such a renewal of manufacturing could just not have been contemplated, let alone executed, during the licence-permit days.

Susim Datta later recounted, 'I would like to believe that, although the initial problems were very large, in the end, this dispersal of the manufacturing facilities helped the company – certainly during the years I was there. It was against this backdrop that HLL settled into a period of growth, an era of mergers and acquisitions (M&As), and a period when there was a lot of media attention on us.'

Another aspect that HLL had to completely reorient in was consumer research. Due to global exposure through media, the consumers were going to change rapidly; their expectations would escalate sharply and market competitors would aggressively track these developments. The expenditure on consumer research thus had to be upped progressively. New techniques like simulated test markets, sequential recycling and qualitative research were implemented.

HLL developed an enormous appetite for organic growth, something which industrial licensing had thwarted for all these years. This aspect of the company did not make newspaper headlines but some of its biggest successes were achieved through organic growth. The company's large detergents division led the charge by adopting a target of making and marketing '1 million tonnes by 1994'. Before liberalisation, the division was selling about 450,000 tonnes. This new ambition and drive to get the growth to reach a million tonnes by 1994 was perceived as big, hairy and audacious. HLL achieved this growth by organic means – by building completely new factories and by backing chosen brands, which included the Wheel detergent bar.

HLL made what I call 'QICA efforts': Quality, Innovation, Collaboration and Acquisitions. The key thing to remember here is that these transformation efforts demanded 'upgrading the engine while the car was running'. These QICA issues will appear to be ordinary when viewed through a contemporary lens, but back then, they were a novel way of thinking. This only reinforces how far Indian management has moved in terms of strategy, in just three decades.

Four of the key initiatives I want to highlight here were:

1. *Quality*: A major product quality drive by benchmarking locally produced products with imports, pointing to the urgent need for upgradation. HLL internally proselytised techniques like TPM, and considered imports of machines and packaging materials as required – something that was nearly impossible before liberalisation.
2. *Innovation*: Next was the special emphasis laid on product innovation and the setting up of a second international research and development (R&D) centre at Bangalore, the first being the one set up in Mumbai in the 1970s.
3. *Collaboration*: HLL got into multifarious business collaborations with its parent company, Unilever. Earlier, brand, technical or service fees could not be remitted to Unilever, but such expenses could now be made under the new regulations. For example, being a global leader in ice creams, Unilever had long been keen on establishing an ice cream business in India. In the licence-permit era, dairy ice cream could only be manufactured on a small scale, being listed as one of some 750 items thus restricted. Labelling its frozen dessert as a 'vegetable fat-based product', Brooke Bond Lipton set up a spanking new investment at Nasik, launching Wall's Frozen Desserts. This was a controversial move at the time, though the turmoil died a natural death

with the subsequent de-reservation of several reservations, including dairy-based ice cream.
4. *Acquisitions*: M&A was a relatively new activity in the 1990s for India Inc. After acquiring Tata Oil Mills Company (TOMCO), HLL went on to acquire Lakmé from Tata after both companies undertook relevant governance processes. HLL also divested its phosphate chemicals business to Tata Chemicals. The acquisition of the public sector company Modern Bakeries followed this move. Later, HLL divested its hair oil brand, Nihar, and purchased an ayurvedic hair oil brand called Indulekha. Cadbury's ice cream operations were acquired by Brooke Bond Lipton. The company entered a hugely complex deal to acquire four independent Kwality ice cream entities, all of which used a common brand name. This was aimed to help Unilever establish an ice cream business in India. The Kissan tomato products business was acquired from Vijay Mallya, as also the Zahura tomato plant from PepsiCo India. It was an appropriate vehicle for the ambitions of Brooke Bond Lipton's foods business.

When I was the managing director of Brooke Bond Lipton, I found a company whose employees had experienced as many as ten mergers within just four years: first, Brooke Bond acquired Lipton, then two tea plantation associates, Doom Dooma Assam and Tea Estates India, followed by Kissan, Milkfood, Zahura and four other Kwality entities. All this was made possible in such a short time because of liberalisation. I might point out here that the resultant company suffered from temporary indigestion and loss of morale during the adjustment period.

In a quandary about how to handle management morale, I casually asked an assistant hailing from Kerala what he thought the future held for the company. Having trained in astrology, he promptly cast the company horoscope after ascertaining its date of birth from the registration certificate and pronounced,

'This company has so far behaved like a man who has given his own name to those he has married. The company will get peace of mind now by behaving like a woman and taking the name of a suitable husband.'

His opinion did not influence the subsequent decision to merge Brooke Bond Lipton into Hindustan Lever, but this became the biggest merger of the time and was also highly controversial, because the company had to face some legal battles.

Before liberalisation, India was quite insulated from global media, trends and thinking. But the changing winds brought global ideas into business. In HLL, this began in the mid-1980s, a tad ahead of liberalisation. HLL strived to be productive, not only in economic terms but also in terms of benefiting the environment. HLL started the first experiment at Chhindwara in Madhya Pradesh, where it began to recycle significant quantities of treated effluent back into process or on land for irrigation. This saved costs for the company while also ensuring that its operations would not place a strain on the rural environment. The chemical engineers in the factories explored the possibility of designing zero-effluent manufacturing facilities long before it became an integral part of sustainability programmes everywhere. Reforestation initiatives at Khamgaon in Maharashtra were also undertaken for similar reasons.

In 1991 HLL earned a revenue of US$700 million, which grew to over US$20 billion around 2022. The company's market capitalisation has grown from US$900 million in 1991 to over US$75 billion in the current times.[7]

It is particularly challenging to lead through times of turbulence. Tata responded to the turmoil caused by the 1991 liberalisation in two ways – first, the company leadership admitted to its limitations and sought outside help, and second, after deep self-reflection, the leadership sought unconventional answers to the company's problems.

Liberalisation and Tata

Just a kilometre away from the HLL office in downtown Mumbai, a newly appointed corporate leader sat in his fourth-floor office at the eponymous Bombay House. On 23 March 1991, the patriarch J.R.D. Tata said to Ratan Tata, 'I have decided to retire and appoint you in my place as the chairman of Tata Sons. I have not decided the date because I have to consult Ajit Kerkar.' Kerkar was the CEO of Taj Hotels, who doubled up as Tata's in-house astrologer. JRD had clearly wanted the day to be an auspicious one, setting a nice example of tradition and modernity coming together!

Ratan Tata had started thinking about transforming the group's operations long before liberalisation. During the 1980s, Ratan Tata had scripted a blueprint for the group, with some estimations about the economy and government policy. Now, ten years after his plan had first been prepared, strengthened with the mantle of leadership and faced with the turbulence of liberalisation, Ratan Tata could explore the prospect of its implementation. Flagship companies, Tata Steel and Tata Motors, had suffered for decades during the licence era due to unjustifiable restrictions on production and pricing, mindless quotas for allocation of resources and severe restrictions on imports. Foreign exchange controls meant that companies had to struggle to convince officials to allow them to import new machinery or deploy state-of-the-art technology; executives found it difficult to even travel abroad on business trips as there was a ceiling on the amount of foreign exchange that could be spent on a per diem basis.

The odds were heavily against the Tata group. Although it had been India's number one group for many decades, it was still small by global standards – lacking in scale, operating mainly in the domestic market – whereas its international competitors had enjoyed the advantage of running operations across the globe. The Tata group was involved in a bewildering assortment of industries and thus lacked focus, thanks to the Monopolies and Restrictive Trade Practices Act (MRTP Act). Most of its revenues and profits were derived from commodity businesses; its own brands – like Hamam and Lakmé – were weak when compared with global brands.

Shackled by an older, slower style of functioning, the Tata group had considerable work to do before it could face fast-paced competition in the future. It was concerned about quality, but given the lack of customer orientation, a mark of the sheltered Indian industry in general, it had to do a lot more to match its more market-savvy rivals. And quality had yet to pervade all aspects of its operations and strategy.

Ratan Tata started holding a series of dinner meetings with his acquaintances at McKinsey. Following this, his leadership team concluded that the group should be restructured (i) to become more competitive; (ii) to provide better returns to the shareholders; and (iii) to be more nimble-footed or more proactive in the changing scene than it had been in the past. These meetings led to the preparation of a set of discussion papers for the Tata Sons board. The plan was to critically look at every company through a group mechanism which did not exist up until that point of time. It should be mentioned that regulations under the MRTP Act had imposed burdens on the group concept over the previous two decades.

It was thus that the Group Executive Office (GEO) was born in 1998, which I joined from my perch as Vice Chairman, HLL. The intention was that the GEO would consist of a group of executive directors of Tata Sons who would hold the responsibility of overseeing the performance of various operating companies. The GEO would also look critically at restructuring the group by way of M&As of our core businesses, and divestment of companies in non-core businesses or markets where Tata did not dominate. Several of these ideas and concepts could not even be considered in earlier years, in the absence of policy liberalisation.

Ratan Tata's first hard decision was regarding TOMCO, which had built a detergent and soap business for the group since 1923. TOMCO had been losing money for some years and it did not quite fit into the Tata view of its own future. Soaps and detergents were, on the other hand, core to HLL. It was, therefore, an opportune moment for the two companies to ink a mutually beneficial agreement. The Tata decision to exit TOMCO and the HLL appetite to acquire it for growth had to pass through complex legal processes. After these, TOMCO was acquired and merged into HLL.

The TOMCO sale was a dramatic development, unimaginable even just a few years previously, in the India of old. Not surprisingly, it emerged as the most newsworthy and sizeable acquisition of the time. There were difficulties galore: the regulatory formalities, getting the proposals passed by the respective boards and appropriately addressing the legal aspects of the merger. It was a crucial turn in the HLL growth story, and just as crucial a step in the Tata divestment approach.

Ratan Tata faced so much criticism for this move from within the group that, as he confessed later, he became hesitant to undertake further divestments. TOMCO's managers received the HLL integration team with considerable suspicion, though the two learned to work collaboratively to see the deal through. The HLL integration team was delighted when Ratan Tata expressed his appreciation for how the team had handled the acquisition.

The Tata group seized the opportunities presented by these reforms and embarked on a remarkable journey that has transformed it into a vibrant and global business house. Tata executed a programme of transformation after liberalisation through four 'welding' mechanisms:
- Setting up the GEO
- Setting up a common, unified brand

- An explicit code of conduct, which had been implicit in earlier years
- A set of operational guidelines for companies that used the brand

The group increased ownership in the major companies and re-established Tata Sons as the focal point of the group, the opposite approach to what J.R.D. Tata had done earlier to comply with the MRTP legislation. Where increase of shareholding was not possible, as in the case of the Associated Cement Company, Tata shareholding was sold off.

Some other group companies were also divested from Tata. There were multiple companies in the same market space, and over time, attempts had been made to rationalise them. Public sector company CMC Ltd was acquired by Tata Consultancy Services (TCS) and later merged into Tata Consultancy.

The implementation of these moves does not mean that these decisions were easily accepted. Each one required a de novo debate with directors of different boards; each one was perceived at the time to be a 'non-Tata way' of solving a problem, and it was only after much cajoling, determination, persuasion and grit that the decisions could be implemented.

The external impression was that Tata was less nimble than others, more resistant to change and extremely set in its ways. Unless Tata companies were benchmarked against the brightest and the best, the probability of change was going to be low. Ratan Tata observed candidly, 'We have yet to seek excellence in all that we do. We hang a picture slightly crooked and live with it for ten years; this should bother us the first time we see it and keep on bothering us until it is set right.'[8]

The Tata group adopted the Tata Business Excellence Model (TBEM), based on the quality improvement framework developed for the Malcolm Baldrige National Quality Awards. In February 1995, the first batch of assessors met at the Tata Management Training Centre for in-depth training on the

Baldrige model. They assessed twelve Tata companies, and the average score was an abysmal 215 out of a maximum score of 1,000 (the major Tata companies have now crossed 600). The journey was to be long, painful, exhausting, but surely rewarding. Implementation required persistence, adaptiveness and resilience – all at once.

The first winner of the JRD Quality Values Award for performance within the TBEM framework was Tata Steel, in 2000. The company went on to win the Deming Prize in 2008 and then the coveted Grand Deming Prize in 2012.

Indeed, TBEM set the tone and created the foundation for a critical transformational exercise in the group. It has also been the glue binding the group together and enhancing the Tata brand.

The opening up of the economy, the removal of unnecessary restrictions relating to investments and the relaxation in foreign exchange rules created new capabilities within Tata companies. Two capabilities are particularly worth mentioning here.

The first is the dramatic restructuring undertaken by Tata Steel during the 1990s. This experience has already been captured earlier in this book. Within a decade, Tata Steel had been transformed by downsizing the workforce to less than half of its starting size. The plan was implemented with empathy and humaneness, symbolic of how to do disagreeable things in an agreeable way. The plants were modernised with new technologies and a new management mindset was instilled, one which could dream up and execute big transformations.

The second was to press ahead with a TCS initial public offering (IPO). This set free an aggressive TCS, then ranked beyond thirtieth among global information technology (IT) players in 2000, to break into the global top ten. The company had worked with Professor Pankaj Ghemawat and had stumbled upon the idea of this audacious goal largely through its internal brainstorming. The company, under the quietly aggressive leadership of its CEO, S. Ramadorai, set about its task through a huge organisational transformation to help its people think about customers, work processes and quality from a global perspective.

If the MRTP Act had continued, Tata could not have implemented its TBEM or the code of conduct. The adherence of Tata companies to both the TBEM process and the Tata Code of Conduct was permanently enshrined in the Brand Equity and Business Promotion Agreement. Each Tata company had to subscribe to this agreement in order to secure the right to use the Tata brand. This played an immense role in presenting to the world Tata products and services that were true reflections of its performance and trust. Beginning with Tata Tea's acquisition of Tetley in 2000, the group made several significant overseas acquisitions.

This eventually led to the formation of the Tata Group Innovation Forum in 2007, and the celebration of the group's pioneering instincts through annual Tata Innovista Awards. The group's increasing number of patent applications reflected the rapid progress that the group was making.

The unshackling of the Indian economy led to dramatic changes within the group, though its core ethos and emphasis on ethical business practices and its commitment to serving the communities in which it operates did not change. The journey since the reforms process began has been exciting for the Tata group. Existing businesses have been rejuvenated, new ones entered into; there has been aggressive expansion into overseas markets and breakthrough products have been launched. The companies in the Tata group are now building the brand of Tata across the globe.

Risks of Transformations

As the reader will have seen, transformations are risky. I reckon the well-known adage of 'no risk no gain' applies with full import here. What are the key risks to be borne in mind by the transformation leadership? There are six major risks worth mentioning here:

(i) The 'demyelination' risk

Have you ever wondered where the expression 'touching a raw nerve' comes from? It refers to the exposed raw nerve when a protective layer in the human body system called myelin gets eroded. Myelin is the fatty protection/insulation around the nerve endings and facilitates fast and efficient transmission of signals. A society or organisation is like the human body. It comprises a complex network of nerve fibres through which communication signals flow. Organisational transformation has the potential to disturb corporate myelin through informal communication channels, water cooler talk and hidden apprehensions. Transformation must do the intended good in the right way, for if done at the wrong time or in the wrong way, even good ideas can misfire.

I will illustrate how demyelination works during transformations, using two examples from the public sphere.

Hindi

As mentioned before, the adoption of Hindi was hugely controversial during the Constituent Assembly debates. During the 1930s, Madras Presidency had been opposed to Hindi. When in the 1950s, the Constitution demanded immediate adoption of Hindi as the sole official language, R.V. Dhulekar of the United Provinces demyelinated people's nerves by making an explosive and ridiculous statement to the effect that people who did not know Hindi had no right to live in India.

Reluctantly, the government decided that English could continue being the official language alongside Hindi until 1965. In 1963, favouring only Hindi was still considered tough, so Nehru announced that the use of English would be extended indefinitely. However, Home Minister Gulzarilal Nanda insisted on accelerating the process of deeming Hindi as the official language of India, and not unexpectedly, Tamil Nadu erupted into riots. Some were of the opinion that this was a local issue for the state to handle. The Central government, however, repealed the 1965 deadline.

Farming

T.T. Krishnamachari, a member of the Constitution Drafting Committee, insisted that agriculture should be an exclusive subject for the Union's political states. Its regional and complex nature made states better custodians of law-making concerning agriculture. His clairvoyance was remarkable. Whatever the intent behind the farm laws of 2017–18 may have been, it was the implementation which has suffered from the poor timing of the decision being announced and the communication gaps within governance systems.

Right after passing three Farm Acts, the Union government imposed restrictions on onion exports, much to the disappointment of Nashik farmers, who enthusiastically eyed soaring prices.

Farming is VUCA – volatile, uncertain, complex, ambiguous – and not independent of economics, sociology, psychology, and above all, politics. For seventy-five years, farming solutions have been piecemeal. For the first time since Independence, the National Democratic Alliance (NDA) government of Prime Minister Atal Bihari Vajpayee published a New Agricultural Policy in 2000. Thereafter, the United Progressive Alliance (UPA) government of Dr Manmohan Singh appointed the Swaminathan Commission, which recommended an updated New Farming Policy in 2006. The fate of its implementation is unknown, but regrettably, the nation has not achieved the aspirational 4 per cent agricultural growth for the last two decades.

In 2020, India announced a New Education Policy, Labour Policy and Science Technology Innovation Policy. A holistic and systems approach had been contemplated in the policy documents of 2000 and 2006. Decisions on complex subjects evolve through experimentation, trial and error. They are not like a win–lose game. In case of misfired decisions, things need to be considered de novo. When one seeks pathways through trial and error, there is no place for personal ego.

Farming unquestionably needs reform in areas which have been explicitly outlined over the years. India is blessed with fine specialists in agriculture, irrigation, economics, but all are trapped within silos of specialisation. By consulting and involving states and farmers, India can better implement a holistic reform for agriculture without danger of demyelination.

(ii) Missing subsonic sounds

When one thinks about organisational transformation, the question that arises is how can a leader know that course correction is required? My answer is that leaders need to listen to the subsonic echoes from the cliffs of their organisation. Each organisation has a unique geology, conditioned by its history and culture. The leader must understand the unique contours of their organisation and let subsonic signals influence their decisions and executive actions. This is difficult to do.

On 29 June 1997, a race was held to celebrate the centenary of the Royal Pigeon Racing Association. More than 60,000 homing pigeons were released at 6.30 a.m. from a field in Nantes, Southern France, flying to lofts all over southern England, 400 to 500 miles away. By 11 a.m., most of the racing birds had made it out of France and were flying over the English Channel. They should have arrived at their lofts by early afternoon. But they did not, and the unfortunate death of so many pigeons was a disaster.

A researcher at the US Geological Survey, Jonathan Hagstrum, proposed a novel explanation. At 11 a.m., when the racing pigeons were crossing the Channel, a Concorde supersonic airliner was flying along its morning flight route from Paris to New York. Such a plane generates a subsonic shockwave – a carpet of sound almost 100 miles wide. This caused the pigeons – that navigate using subsonic sounds – to lose their bearings.

In every organisation, there are edges and cliffs from which subsonic echoes of transformation emanate. Those echoes are faint, but the astute manager must strain to catch the message. Leaders must listen to this infrasound to avoid losing their orientation – like the pigeons did in the race.

The evolution of liberalisation in India is instructive. The thinking and planning really started during Indira Gandhi's prime ministerial tenure in 1980, but could not be fleshed out in its entirety due to her sudden assassination. Her son, Rajiv Gandhi, stepped into her shoes and gave the strategy a fresh start but was soon embroiled in controversy. When P.V. Narasimha Rao finally became prime minister in June 1991, reform enthusiasts wanted him to go for the Big Bang approach, as such approaches are usually very visible. He chose the middle path, which he in fact articulated at the Tirupati Congress. He reaffirmed his commitment to Nehru's ideas, even though he went on to approve a completely different course of action a short while later.

Another example was Operation Flood, which ushered in a dairy revolution in India. It owes some fillip to a visit by Prime Minister Lal Bahadur Shastri to Anand in the 1960s. He expressed the desire that instead of staying at Dr Kurien's house – his host – since there were no hotels or guest houses in Anand at the time, he spend the night at a farmer's house in Kaira district. This caused great consternation among security personnel and logistical complications for the administration.

To keep this a secret, a village farmer was initially told that two foreigners would stay with him and only at the last minute was he told that his guests were going to be the prime minister and the Gujarat chief minister. Shastri ji had an early dinner with the nervous farmer and then went around the village, talking to the people. Most of the villagers kept awake through the night as Shastri ji went about his enquiries and visits to the colony of Harijans, Muslims and all the other communities. Everywhere, he enquired about the milk cooperative they were members of. This went on from 8 p.m. to 2 a.m.

The next morning, he asked Dr Kurien to explain the secret of Amul's success when nowhere else in the country had cooperatives worked. Dr Kurien explained the ground realities succinctly. Shastri ji had taken the time to learn what he could not have through many seminars, sitting in Delhi. It was a unique approach for a modern leader to listen to the infrasound of what really mattered to dairy farmers.

Authority and the trappings of power often plug leaders' ears. Listening carefully is such an elementary lesson – why would one need to explain its importance? It is precisely because it is elementary and some of life's biggest mistakes are made by ignoring the elementary!

Leo Tolstoy opened *Anna Karenina* with, 'Happy families are all alike; each unhappy family is unhappy in its own way.' Likewise, all change management cases resemble each other, but the issues of each one are unique to the concerned organisation's culture, beliefs and mindsets. Listening carefully to the unique infrasound of one's organisation is a valuable tool.

(iii) Capacity for change
I place great emphasis on a leader's need to possess both discipline and creativity to execute a change programme successfully. There is a delicate balance between an organisation's capacity and the leader's vision for change. The viability of a company's transformation effort depends on its unique experiences and culture. In the rush to implement change, leaders often unleash multiple change initiatives. What worked for Unilever or General Electric may well fail when implemented at a public sector undertaking – and vice versa. To mention one example,

Unilever's 'Path to Growth' multiple change initiative in 1999 did not work well, as admitted by the company's top leadership in 2004.[9]

The first task for a new leader – whether internally or externally hired – is to assess an organisation's capacity for change. This requires keeping up a connection with people and listening rather than speaking, while also reflecting on the nuances of various conversations to ferret out any hidden messages.

When I became chairman of Unilever Arabia in 1991, I wrongly assumed that Unilever had a global style of working, and that HLL represented that style. I soon learned that while there were indeed standard Unilever processes, working behaviours varied in Arabia, India, Sweden, France and Netherlands. The multinational team spotted several differences in working behaviour compared to their home countries. They were excited by the novel opportunity to discover fresh approaches which were quite different from past experiences.

Then, there is the vision for change which needs to be considered.

Initially, I had the old-fashioned mindset that I would create an Arabian version of HLL, but it turned out to be a silly way to frame my vision as a leader. I needed to be patient and not impose my ideas on the new team. I undertook painstaking efforts to consult with the teams and to chisel out a collective plan, shaped by their ideas. This threw up a high-octane plan for the organisation to double dollar sales within four years and dollar profits within three years. Luckily, the goal was achieved. It rocked the company boat without sinking it. For me, there were two overarching lessons here.

First, the acceptance that there inevitably were multiple visions and that mine was just one such vision. Each employee's vision is based on the six lenses through which that employee views his or her own life and career, as I have written in my book, *Six Lenses* – purpose, authenticity, courage, trust, luck and fulfilment. Unless people's lenses are focused on the same vision, the organisation cannot work on one harmonised vision.

Another lesson was that persuading others becomes easier when one allows oneself to be persuaded by them. The noted organisational psychologist at Wharton Adam Grant has suggested three approaches:[10]

1. When you must persuade a know-it-all character, he suggests asking the know-it-all to explain how things work. Think about how Hanuman persuaded Sita in the Ashoka Vana that he was authentic and not a demon-imposter.
2. Let the stubborn person seize the opportunity and give vent to their need to maintain a sense of control. Ask questions instead of giving answers – this can effectively lower people's guards.
3. Find the right way to praise the narcissist. Recall how Vibhishana praised Ravana before attempting to dissuade him from killing Hanuman. Praise is a powerful antidote to a narcissist's insecurity, provided the praise is regarding an area that is different from the matter at hand. Vibhishana praised Ravana's erudition before persuading him to review his proposed punishment to Hanuman!

Additionally, listen to Julia Dhar's talk.[11] She outlines three ideas: first, let the instinct of curiosity exceed the instinct of clash. You can say something like, 'Oh, I never thought of the subject that way. Tell me more.' Second, enter the conversation with the attitude of adaptation rather than victory, a bit like how a rock climber's approach is different from a marathoner's. Third and last, check that you are anchored with the other person on purpose – are you both even trying to solve the same problem?

(iv) Inattentional blindness

I now focus on inattentional blindness due to one of two obsessions: predetermined signals or self-obsession. This occurs when you are so intensely focused on the signals you are looking for that you miss other vital signals. It could also be because of an obsession with the self, for example, Adolf Hitler, who was singularly obsessed with expanding *lebensraum* while enhancing his personal image through dress and highly rehearsed demagoguery.

In a 1999 university experiment, respondents were asked to count the number of times the ball changed hands during the replay of a basketball match. Amid the frames, significant nine-second interruptions – irrelevant to the basketball game – were interposed, showing a big gorilla thumping his chest. Many observers completely missed the multiple appearances of the gorilla since their brain was so focused on the assigned task of counting the exchanges of the ball.

An example from the cell phone industry further illustrates this point. Motorola made the first cell phones. Company leaders were so focused on existing telecom customers that they completely missed the '"gorilla" of their customers' customers'. Nokia took the market by storm next. Later, Nokia too lost its lead because of its inattentional blindness to further technological developments.

Here is an example of a great chemical company, Imperial Chemical Industries (ICI), to illustrate how strong technological professionals missed the signals from a very different field when danger was emanating from beyond the industry. ICI was a fantastic company full of bright technical professionals. It had developed and owned more than 33,000 patents. The flip side was that its leaders treated the securities markets with disdain. In 1991, the Hanson Group, through its merchant bank, Smith New Court, bought a 2.8 per cent stake worth GBP 240 million in ICI. The company was thereafter caught in inattentional blindness due to its beliefs and began its descent. It is now part of Akzo Nobel, but a pale force in global business.

The South Indian tea plantation industry makes for another example. India had long been the world's largest tea producer and exporter, while Sri Lanka was a much smaller producer, though it gradually became a major exporter since their domestic market was small. South Indian teas and Sri Lankan teas had some similarity in tea types and quality. From the 1970s, Russia became a major buyer of South Indian teas under the rupee/rouble trade agreement. Russians bought humongous quantities at unrealistic prices because it was a managed trade, not a free trade. The South Indian industry thereby lost its focus on quality and began chasing production volume blindly. The labour unions and the state governments of Kerala and Tamil Nadu also insisted that the wages and amenities for plantation workers be increased rapidly. This continued until the early 1990s, when, with economic liberalisation, it started to become obvious that South Indian teas would soon be outclassed in quality as well as price. The industry had suffered from inattentional blindness, and it took a decade of battling decline before plantation companies started to address the core issues at hand.

Anyone can self-test for inattentional blindness as a leader by reflecting on six key questions:

i. Do I feel that many people are out to block my initiatives and dynamism?
ii. Do people fawn over me?
iii. Do my colleagues feel free to offer different views or express a contrarian view?
iv. Do I feel a bit cut off from people and hence from reality?
v. Have I made special efforts to connect with the remote parts of my organisation?
vi. When I do connect, does my visit appear stage-managed?

The answers offer tell-tale signals. Blaming past leaders and imaginary enemies is a sign of incompetence and insecurity – leading to rhetoric and rabble-rousing. Such people are vulnerable to inattentional blindness.

(v) Slow down to go faster

Transformational leaders chart out the four stages of start → roadmap → time plan → end point. The initial stages are generally planned well, while the later stages demand flexibility. Execution requires constant review and adjustment, failing which, two risks arise: initiative overload and declaration of victory. Here are a couple of examples to illustrate this further:

Initiative overload

Leaders might assume that the speed of change is achieved by mounting more and more initiatives. A Bain & Company partner, Jenny Davis-Peccoud, wrote a great piece titled 'The Company Cure for Initiative Overload',[12] wherein she explains how the post-mortem of several disasters or failures in corporate transformation reveals initiative overload as a contributor. A good example is the manner in which successive governments treated the erstwhile public sector Air India, until Tata reclaimed the company in 2023.

Early declaration of victory

In 2003, the 'India Shining' campaign worth INR 150 crore was launched by an overenthusiastic NDA to declare the success of their initiatives. The celebratory tone lacked credibility to such an extent that the NDA lost the 2004 elections. Another example demonstrates this early victory malaise. In 2017, author Quint Studer wrote about how a Chicago 'Great Comeback' hospital declared victory at the first taste of success. The very next month, the hospital had to retract its self-celebratory accolades. Harvard Business School (HBS) Professor John Kotter has written in the *Harvard Business Review* on why transformation efforts fail by declaring victory too soon. Leaders like to come across as encouraging to their audience by reassuring them that the challenge is being addressed head-on. That may result in less diligence and some complacency. Perhaps these are the reasons for not announcing victory too soon.

(vi) A non-scientific temper

Scientific temper is not about science. It demands an attitude of curiosity, dissent and debate. Think back to how epidemics ended in the past – none was eradicated within a short time frame. The *Boston Review* tellingly reported in its 'Science and Technology' column: 'The history of epidemic endings has taken many forms, and only a handful of them have resulted in the elimination of a disease ... The two faces of an epidemic, the biological and the social, are closely intertwined, but they are not the same ... science is deeply contingent upon local practices.'[13]

While the report emphasises the intersection of science with society, leaders may fall into the trap of excluding both science and social aspects during decision-making. In transformation, you need both STEM and SHAPE: Science, Technology, Engineering and Manufacturing must be combined with Social Sciences, Humanities, Arts, People and Economy. This is why I advocate thinking slowly and deeply.

A Korean proverb says, 'It is when you are in a rush that you have to slow down.' Vedanta advises using the intellect over just the mind, through *shravanam* (listening), *mananam* (thinking) and *nidhidhyasanam* (introspecting).

Here are two examples from the business world. Unilever's 'Path to Growth' was announced in 1999. Intense programmes followed, leaving employees in a tizzy. Till 2004, however, the targets were still not met. Soon, top management and business targets both had to be revised.

In 1992, Arthur Martinez was selected to lead the American retail chain Sears against competition from entrants like Walmart. For two years, Martinez introduced on a slew of strategic initiatives, leaving the company employees rather breathless. He then declared the turnaround complete and successful. Soon thereafter, the company faltered, and Martinez had to step down in 1999.

An example from public life in Ecuador is terrifyingly instructive. Jamil Mahuad was an immensely successful mayor of Quito from 1992 to 1998. He was popular, he walked around the city to meet his voters and decentralised problem-solving by motivating citizens to solve their own problems. After declaring the success of his Quito model, he got elected as president. In this new position, Jamil could not replicate his personal contact activities. Gradually, he grew distant. He relied on his aides to report problems and recommend solutions to him. Urgent actions were required for the mounting problems of inflation, foreign debt, bankruptcy of banks and devastation from an unexpected El Niño storm. In a dramatic move, Jamil froze bank accounts and 'dollarised' the economy. The economy did not respond positively to this move. People came out on the streets, and in January 2000, a coalition of military officers forced Jamil out of office.

Such are the travails of adopting a non-scientific temper – it can trap the leadership in initiative overload, declaring victory too soon, or failing to slow down to move fast.

In the next chapter, we will review why transformation and pain are constant companions – while this pain can be minimised, it cannot be eliminated.

Summary

- Organisational transformations can be transactional or strategic.
- It is important to develop and nurture a collective legend about the future.
- Though you have no control over it, luck does play some role in the outcomes of transformation efforts, especially unearned luck.

- General lessons can be extracted from the experiences of HLL's and Tata's responses to liberalisation.
- While executing transformations, it is important to bear in mind the six major risks.

3

Pain

Endurance and Inevitability

Organisational transformations are gut-wrenching and painful, and there is no shortcut. Do not believe the many books promoting painless transformational change for organisations. A leader may be able to work to minimise the pain caused by this change, but not eliminate it. In fact, it often appears that the leadership team must voluntarily seek out the pain to drive transformation.

Pain is inevitable and there are both rational explanations and reasons for this.

First, every organisation carries an institutional memory, which is passed on to employees as 'the way things are done here'. This institutional memory can be powerful, but may also be a hindrance. The story of how the institutional memory of Kodak hindered its evolution from photographic film to keep pace with emerging digital technologies has been told many times. The Kodak Brownie camera was a legendary brand for several decades.

Another oft-quoted example is the institutional memory of the Ford Motor Company. The company became hugely successful by practising the eponymous Henry Ford's statement, 'The customer can have any colour of car so long as it is black.' When General Motors segmented the automotive market in the 1920s with design and colour, Ford lost US auto market leadership, never to regain it.

Second, organisations have a limited absorptive capacity for change, just as doctors understand how patients have different capacities for tolerating pain. Organisations suffer from fear of change to fatigue from change. Under the much-idolised Jack Welch, General Electric underwent huge change during the 1980s and 1990s, making it a billion-dollar corporation with US$600 billion of market capitalisation. After 2010, the stresses on the company increased manyfold and its market capitalisation collapsed to US$60 billion! Its absorptive capacity limited avenues for further transformation while maintaining its status as a conglomerate. So the company had to be broken into parts.

Third, while management consultants do play a constructive role, increasingly, operating leaders tend to 'outsource' their transformation strategies and execution to these consultants. Consultancy companies add great value, but only if the client uses them in the right manner, rather than abdicating tasks to the consultant which are beyond their skill set. When such companies are used as a 'viatical' – a parallel adjunct of the client company – then the inadvertent consequence is that the client company gets hollowed out, losing its own managerial capabilities. In their book *The Big Con*, Mariana Mazzucato and Rosie Collington point out how America's NASA and Britain's NHS achieved short-term cost savings through cost-reduction programmes undertaken with consultants, but ended up hollowing out the internal managerial capabilities in several ways. In my experience, the fault lies with the client and not the consultant in these cases.

The reality is that the above-mentioned reasons serve to exacerbate the pain of organisational transformation.

Lessons from Nature

How exactly does metamorphosis occur in nature? Several years ago, while writing my first book, I was in search of a metaphor for organisational transformation. I found one in nature.

Butterflies are good ecological indicators. I learned a lot from my periodic visits to the Nilgiris. In 1986, a scientist and conservationist called Torben Larsen conducted a butterfly survey of the Nilgiris and identified 301 varieties of butterflies that exist in the mountain ranges.[1] In 2018 the Tamil Nadu Forest Department conducted another survey and added three new varieties.

The *Scientific American* of 10 August 2012 lucidly explains the process of metamorphosis – the ultimate analogy for transformation in nature – and I was reminded of a start-up after reading the article. A caterpillar overfeeds and stocks up on nutrients and then digests its own body into a soup rich with enzymes. This digestion process leaves behind what looks like an amorphous mess, but that is not what it is. Certain groups of cells survive because they contain the genetic code to grow back the body parts required for a mature life later. These cells, called 'imaginal discs', help the animal reconstruct its anatomy with wings and muscles to break through the cocoon and emerge as a breathtakingly beautiful butterfly.[2]

Let us apply these lessons from nature to companies. The equivalent of imaginal discs is the embedded organisational culture – the unique characteristics of mindsets, behaviours and actions that define the very being of the company and must be preserved. Do all start-ups think about the imaginal discs that they must embed into their company in the early stages? How many voluntarily subject themselves to a self-digestion process after they have engorged themselves with growth lessons over a long period? Very few, I reckon, and that is one important reason why the survival rate among startups is so low.

Think of grown-up companies for whom such 'creative destruction' is essential to survive and prosper in the long term. The dramatic transformations of Gap (records to apparel), Netflix (DVD rentals to streaming), Tiffany (stationery to jewellery) are worth noting. IBM subjected itself to a self-digestive transformation process in the 1990s, which is so well described in Louis Gerstner's book, *Who Says Elephants Can't Dance?*[3] The company survived, though it is reported to have again lost the plot in recent decades. Apple went through something similar in 1997, but the company recovered from its mistakes. However, companies like Kodak, Enron and Lehman Brothers, etc. did not. Their narratives are now a part of business archives.

Jamsetji Tata began his enterprise as a trading and textile company. For growth, he expanded into steel manufacturing and hydropower generation. For culture, he embedded the mindset and behaviour of social responsibility (imaginal discs) by, inter alia, endowing the Indian Institute of Science. A famous statement of his goes, 'In a free enterprise, the community is not just another stakeholder in the business, but, in fact, the very purpose of its existence.'[4]

His successor, Dorabji, brought to fruition the unfulfilled ambitions of his father in steel manufacturing and hydropower generation before he diversified into cement, construction, banking, insurance and allied areas. The imaginal discs of corporate philanthropy were strengthened by investments in cancer research and a hospital, among other initiatives.

Future successors, notably J.R.D. Tata, expanded the enterprise into aviation, chemicals, truck-making and thermal power. Through the century, textiles got de-emphasised, as the company shifted focus from trading to manufacturing. Their entry into the financial services business was overtaken by regulatory events. The imaginal discs of social commitment were strengthened through long-term modification of the companies' articles of association, and the establishment of the Tata Institute of Fundamental Research (TIFR), the Tata Institute of Social Sciences (TISS) and the National Centre for the Performing Arts (NCPA).

In recent decades, the group exited textiles, cement, soaps and a few other industries. They also globalised the business and entered futuristic fields like IT, communications, electronics and electric vehicles. Their imaginal discs were strengthened through increased funds for furthering the social agenda of Tata Trusts, promoting a national chain of cancer hospitals and the impactful deployment of their corporate social responsibility funds.

While these developments may read like a list of their accomplishments, they are mere dots in their history. I can state from experience that the process was slow and painful. The inevitable reduction of the portfolio was indeed painful, and the new portfolio grew out of the entrepreneurial moves. All through the century and more, Tata's imaginal discs helped in promoting the enterprise and strengthening its distinctive culture of community orientation. But no transformation can happen without pain.

Perceptions Are Important

Transformation leaders need to have generalist skills and don't necessarily have to be specialists. Leaders desire that the execution of their change programme is perceived to be predictable and well thought out, but in practice, a semblance of order is accompanied by lots of chaos. Uncertainty is an essential part of transformation. For animals, uncertainty is a way of life. When faced with danger, both humans and animals realign their internal resources to meet the oncoming challenge – the fight-or-flight response. In general, however, human beings tend to yearn for predictability far more than animals.

Here is an example: cave crickets live in extreme conditions of darkness and dampness. Hence, they are usually eyeless. To survive and grow, they develop feelers which are four times the length of their body. This enables them to feel their way around the dark cave they reside in. Now imagine a human being whose legs and arms can reach 20–25 feet around them!

A transforming organisation may start out as highly focused, but getting muddled up and having to adapt is inevitable. A leader may choose to disregard stakeholders' views or sentiments, but being mindful about stakeholders is not optional. Transformation agendas need continuous recalibration, based on signals. Apart from the court of law, the court of public opinion also matters. Optics are important, though optics may not always dictate a leader's actions and the courts of law and public opinion may well be divergent, sometimes.

A popular perception is that US 'lost' the Vietnam War. The fact is that the US lost 58,220 soldiers as opposed to over 1 million Viet Cong casualties.[5] However, the residual optics of the 1968 Tet Offensive created the lasting legend that the US lost the war.

An example from the business world, Nestlé India lacked antennas in the early stages of the Maggi noodles crisis. Suresh Narayanan, Chairman of Nestlé India, was brought back to India from an overseas posting. He described at public presentations how he went about setting up the required antennas to feel the right way forward for the company. The response packaged together both the order and chaos.[6]

The United Breweries (UB) Group of companies has gone through dramatic growth and transformation in the last twenty years. About seven years ago, Kingfisher, a UB company, defaulted on repayment of bank loans and failed to pay employee salaries. Meanwhile, Chairman Vijay Mallya's birthday celebration in Goa caught media attention. While, technically speaking, the shareholder liability is limited to the share capital and Mallya was fully entitled to spend his personal wealth however he wished, the optics were unfavourable for the company. In the court of public opinion, Vijay Mallya stood 'condemned'.

The telecom industry in India underwent dramatic transformation during the last thirty years. Convulsions occurred every few years from the early days of Minister Sukhram to the 2G episode. The 2G controversy was settled through the long-winded process of law. However, in the court of public opinion, the UPA lost the case much earlier. Optics are important.

Farm bills were hurried through in 27 days – from introduction of the bills to presidential assent. The average time for passage of bills is 150 days. Protagonists credibly argue that the process was legitimate because 'an elected government took it through parliament'. But, in the court of public opinion, the bills were not accepted, as evidenced by the prolonged protests by farmers, apart from the paralysis of implementation.

Recall that a magnificent Delhi Durbar was held three times – in 1877, 1903 and 1911. The first two were lavish coronation events of absent British monarchs; they were held while Indians faced a massive famine and thousands of citizens were in relief camps.

Perceptions are thus an important consideration for businesses.

Competitors Must Compete but Can Also Collaborate

Particularly when a crisis is large, competitive players must consider collaborating. Whenever I mention this, the responses I get are interesting. They range from 'great idea' to 'theoretical' to 'there is no real-life example of competitors cooperating'. From my repertoire of stories on collaborative competitors, I shall offer some examples. In these times of increasingly competitive politics and enterprises, there are relevant lessons to be learnt.

Politics and business are really not the same as war. They are not games with winners and losers. A 'China-free world' or a 'Republican-free America' are both silly ideas. Unfortunately, a motivational narrative has developed that not only is winning all-important but quashing one's competitors is equally important to manage future threat.

Somerset Maugham famously said, 'It is not enough to succeed, others must fail.' A version of this was made memorable during the 1996 Olympics by the Nike Air television advertisement, starring basketball player Lisa Leslie: 'You don't win silver, you lose gold.' The new mantra for ecommerce start-ups is 'winners take all', as is announced periodically. New unicorns with irrational valuations crop up at regular intervals and subsequent misfortunes among them causes some analysts to express economic concerns. Valuation, as is practised, is more an art than a science and depends on the future view of the valuer.

Politics and business are not about annihilating competition either. They are not zero-sum games, as pointed out by Simon Sinek.[7] Many areas of human endeavour involve multiple interdependent variables. Simple decisions that ignore the total system effect are often counterproductive.

Five important lessons for engaging in successful co-opetition:

(i) Do not lose time in proving that a crisis is unique and rare. Every crisis is unique and rare.

(ii) Do not waste time finding out who is at fault. Act fast and with a strong feedback loop to correct inevitable mistakes.

(iii) Bring in accomplished, experienced generalist leaders to sort out the problem, not just domain or technical specialists.

(iv) Focus on communication with employees, who are bound to feel insecure. Exhort, persuade, cajole players that cooperation can expand the pie for all. Later, competition will determine how to divvy up the expanded pie. Some players might act out of line, but many might heed.

(v) Be respectful and invoke the help of the whole ecosystem – government machinery, employees, customers, players and bureaucrats. For example, in the Satyam resolution, key players were Secretary, Company Affairs, Anurag Goel, Nasscom President Som Mittal, HDFC Chairman Deepak

Parekh, bureaucrats C. Achuthan and T.N. Manoharan, to name just a few.

Here are some more examples of co-opetition. In 1982, Lipton India was in a financial crisis. As its only competitor at that time, Brooke Bond India was concerned. The latter's chairman, C.S. Samuel, persuaded Lipton India's majority shareholder, Unilever, to not close down the company as it was a competitive thorn at that time in the side of Brooke Bond India. Why would Samuel do what he did? Because he understood well that his company needed the competition from Lipton. Similarly, in 2005, Toyota Motors Chairman Hiroshi Okuda took positive steps to save former market leader General Motors from the combined onslaught of Toyota, Honda and Nissan in the US automobile market.

In India's current telecom market, can three players show such statesmanship?

Recall the summer of 1996, when the shaky Narasimha Rao government felt compelled by national interest to buy Sukhoi-30 aircraft from Russia. Journalist Shekhar Gupta has narrated how, through deft interventions and collaborative consultations, political arch-rivals collaborated – Congress's Narasimha Rao, Bharatiya Janata Party's Jaswant Singh and Atal Bihari Vajpayee, and Samajwadi Party's Mulayam Singh – to avert public controversy.

Similarly, biographer and historian Dr Dorothy Kearns Goodwin has documented how the American Republic in the 1860s was saved by Abraham Lincoln through cooperation with his political rivals.[8]

Why Do Large Organisations Go Around in Circles?

By nature, the problems that top managers and leaders face are very often foggy and unclear. In their pursuit of efficiency, managers sometimes lose effectiveness. Are efficiency and effectiveness different?

The code of an efficient organisation is:
- You work on things you understand quite well.
- You plan in detail and review actions against that plan.
- You impose a process and responsibility.
- You expect completion as per an agreed timetable.
- You would throw resources to accomplish the tasks.

The code of an effective organisation is:
- You work on things you don't quite understand.
- You find it difficult to plan in any detail as the way forward is unclear.
- You try out approaches and adjust your plans flexibly.
- You expect progress, but are not sure of completion.
- You must generate new options continuously, not just place more resources.

Leaders cannot choose whether to be efficient or effective; they must strive for both. Since effectiveness is essential, they have to opt for a path which is inefficient to accomplish the task.

The most efficient path between two points is a straight line. Then why does the housefly approach its target in a spiralling circle? Given its eye and body structure, the fly must adapt itself to reach its goal in a way that is effective, even though it is not the most efficient way. The fly has two eyes, which are so large that they cover most of its head. The fly can simultaneously see above, below, in front and behind it. Each of the fly's eyes is made up of about 2,000 tiny, hexagonally packed lenses. No two lenses point in the same direction. Not only that, each lens operates independently of the others. The consequence of this 360-degree vision is that a fly-eye view of the world is highly fractured; it cannot easily adjust to see distance or detailed patterns and shapes. Hence, the fly does not have sharp vision. Everything it sees appears blurred in its compound eye, as opposed to the simple human eye, which sees one unified image. The fly's approach spiral is the most effective way for it to narrow down onto its target.

As the fly approaches an object, the image shifts slightly in each facet. To hold its vision of the object in a constant position, the fly must adjust its whole body. At each turn of its body, the fly is closer to the object, so the radius of the circle of approach progressively becomes smaller and smaller. If one plots the approach path of the fly, it will resemble a coil or a spiral with a decreasing radius.

Maybe this applies to organisation leaders as well. When people are thinking, there is bound to be a diversity of views. An organisation is the sum total of these diverse viewpoints. Differing viewpoints lead to differing agendas and these naturally serve as a source of potential conflict among its people. This can impede or sour the relationships between various actors and players.

A further complexity comes from the fact that people in the organisation may or may not express their genuine view in a formal forum. If the view expressed at the table is different from the real view that the person holds, there is a further increase in the complexity. That is why any organisation that has a truly compound eye has a very complex agenda to tackle.

Like the fly, the anatomy of the organisation's eye prevents a sharp vision from guiding its movement. The lack of a sharp vision prevents it from moving in a straight line, the most efficient path. It thus has to assess its distance from the goal, make a move, reassess distance, adjust its position again and keep repeating that process till it reaches its goal – much like the fly.

It is the paramount role of leadership to sharpen the organisation's vision, but that does not necessarily happen efficiently. The leader cannot drive the organisation to move in a straight line to what he thinks is the most logical solution. In fact, it would probably be correct to say that while solving complex issues, going around in circles is the more efficient mode of functioning because it is more effective. The more complex the problem, the more likely it is that the effective solution will require the leadership to move in circles, rather than a straight line.

The English moralist Samuel Johnson perceived the world as a 'tangled, teeming jungle of plots, follies, vanities, and egoistic passions in which anyone – the innocent and virtuous no less than the vicious – is likely to be ambushed'. That is why we need to accept the reality that the human mind is 'a noisy parliament of competing factions'. Yet all our training tells us to plan for efficient outcomes and expect the organisation to move along a straight line.

The greatest source of employees' exasperation is often that their 'leaders do not seem to do what is obvious'.

Summary

- Transformation and pain are constant companions.
- Perceptions of what is changing about an organisation are as important as the change itself.
- The larger the organisation, the greater is its propensity to go around in circles. Leaders seek a balance between efficiency – for which they are trained – and effectiveness, for which they are paid.

4

Leadership

Followers and Leaders

Transformation of organisations is generally perceived as leader-initiated and leader-led. This is true, but there can be no transformation, leadership or change if there are no willing and motivated followers in tow.

To be future-ready, an organisation must have positive recruitment practices and talent bench strength, while having top leaders who practise great leadership development processes. In this chapter, the initial issue of talent bench strength is addressed; this is followed by CEO leadership development practices. Together, these are crucial to successful transformation management.

Talent Bench Strength

Sustainable talent management is an infinite game

We celebrate the success of Indian CEOs who have made it big in international companies. Apart from business managers, kudos and encomiums are also due to the academics, doctors and scientists who have deservedly begun to receive international recognition. While the leaders have great merit, we cannot overlook the role played by meritocracy in countries that encourage great talent to flower.

So far as management is concerned, I have a deep interest – partly because of my professional background and partly because of my passionate belief that talent and management excellence are *the most important* ingredients of SHE (sustainable, honest and enlightened) enterprises. SHE companies are crucial for the advancement of our nation. Every nation has developed by building great enterprises. The track record of talent management among many companies, both established and start-ups, suggests that India can do better. Just six generations ago, there was no concept of an Indian manager. A brief history of the factors that led to the establishment and growth of Indian management talent is both instructive and inspirational, so I shall attempt it.

Circa 1800, India was numbered among the richest nations in the world in terms of GDP, which is why the Dutch, the English and the French were all eager to trade with India. This is what led to colonisation. Textiles, spices, ivory and agricultural commodities were all hugely valuable trading items. The Industrial Revolution in England led to employment generation in mining, manufacturing, railways and postal services, among many other industries. Apart from workers, the tribe of managers also started to develop around this time. For their own interests, the British colonialists introduced infrastructural activities in India, their most prized colony. In the initial decades, experienced British workers and technicians worked in India as supervisors or managers. The activity reserved for the natives within India or other colonies in Africa, West Indies, Guyana, or Fiji, was unskilled labour.

Historians credit Dadabhai Naoroji for mooting and advocating the idea that 'natives' had to be trained and deployed to take on the administrative challenges of a complex country like India. As a British parliamentarian, Naoroji lobbied for the Indian Civil Service (ICS) to admit suitable Indians. His mission was met with initial success when Indians were allowed to sit for the ICS exam, but the exam was conducted only in London. He then pushed for the ICS entrance exam to be held in India, concurrently with the exam in London. Several years later, this became standard practice. It was in this manner that Indians were groomed to serve as ICS officers in India.

Meanwhile, railways and postal services started to be established in India as well. Progressively, Indians started to enter the defence forces as juniors. Private entrepreneurs took to modern industry, particularly in the domains of textiles, jute, coal, steel and tea, to name a few. All such activities required administrative and management talent. Indians joined as junior staff members and a few grew to occupy junior managerial roles. This was true right into the 1930s.

International companies also began to develop the Indian market for their products. British American Tobacco, the original promoter of what is ITC today, started to set up distribution networks for cigarettes throughout India.

Unilever started to manufacture its globally famous Sunlight and Lifebuoy soaps and exported its products to India from the 1880s. Thereafter, Unilever set up local manufacturing facilities in the 1930s. To make, distribute and sell, young British managers were deputed initially to appoint wholesalers in towns all over India, from within trading communities. A senior Unilever officer called Andrew Knox, then chairman of what was called 'the overseas committee', wrote a report in the early 1930s. This report now lies in the Unilever archives. In it, Knox recorded his view that Unilever should 'Indianise' the management to develop the Indian market. Either he was a visionary or just a shrewd observer. That is exactly what the global company started to do, soon after. The first Indian 'covenanted manager' to be recruited was Prakash Tandon, in 1937.

Among international companies, Unilever identified and developed Indian managers from the mid-1930s onwards. They did it so well that today, after several decades, HUL-recruited Indians occupy top positions in the global corporation. Arguably, Unilever has been the most successful among all companies in talent development. In the last few decades, at any point of time, the Indian subsidiary had 150–200 managers on secondment to other geographies in which Unilever operated. The author has benefited from such secondment as well, when I was posted to head the Unilever subsidiary in the Arabian Peninsula several decades ago.

Dadabhai Naoroji's pursuit of recruiting Indians into the civil service resulted in Satyendranath Tagore, brother of the illustrious poet Rabindranath Tagore, joining the ICS around 1864. For the Indian Army, it was a momentous occasion when in 1949 General K.M. Cariappa was appointed as the first Indian to head the force. J.M. Lall became the first Indian CEO of Imperial Chemical Industries in 1959. When Prakash Tandon became the first Indian Chairman of Hindustan Lever in 1961, it was a tribute to the vision of Andrew Knox, and was notable for business management in general.

It was not only international companies that started to take such deliberate steps to develop domestic talent. Indian entrepreneurs also started to hone their own ambitions. Textile mills came up in Bombay and Ahmedabad. Jute mills were set up in undivided Bengal. Tea plantations and factories were established in Assam, Kerala and Tamil Nadu. Tata set up a steel plant and hydroelectric power stations. All of them either recruited foreigners for technical help or trained their own manpower. These Indian entrepreneurs were focused on developing Indian managerial talent.

As can be seen from this brief review, talent management has been a complex and long journey, demanding great persistence and patience. Talent management represents the 'infinite game', to borrow Sinek's term.

Talent is tougher to build than factories

Talent building is an infinite game, but how long and difficult is it?

Efficient factories are daunting to build. First come land assessment, acquisition and preparation. Second come technology selection, equipment purchase, layout and installation. The third and toughest part is manpower planning, employee recruitment, and most importantly, skilling, training and building motivation to deliver. Fourth comes the grand concertino of assembling the parts of the jigsaw, before finally commissioning the factory. Thereafter, a fifth challenge is the operation of the new plant on an optimum basis to ensure efficiency and effectiveness. All this can take a decade – maybe more.

An experienced manufacturing/project manager will confirm that the first two of the above five steps follow the logic or science of engineering. But the last three concern people and abide by the art of human engineering: how to recruit, train and continuously motivate people for quality and productivity improvement.

To build and sustain a company management cadre from top leadership downwards is both difficult and time-consuming. The talent process involves the rather imprecise art of judging how to develop human beings – from recruitment to evaluation; from creating talent density to achieving talent portability; from defining what a manager's responsibility is to hold the manager accountable; and finally, to advance the best talent out of a well-honed bench strength. These processes do not have a direct cause-and-effect connection, unlike action and reaction in physics. Rather, the response occurs to a series of initiations over a period with the law of unintended consequences at play.

The closest, though imperfect, parallel to leadership development in a company is parenting. As we all know, parenting is a lifelong process. A parent is 24x7 at the job, mentally and psychologically. There is no intermission or remission. Indeed, parents' involvement with the progeny never ceases. Rightly or wrongly, even when the progeny reaches adulthood, parents' care and concern for their well-being continues.

In my experience, the two toughest jobs in the world are excelling at parenting and building leadership talent for the long term. Just like parenting cannot and should not be left to just one parent or to grandparents, talent development cannot and must not be left exclusively to either HR or to the CEO. Talent development is a core part of the responsibilities of any manager. The distinguishing mark of a fine company is the glorious *jugalbandi* (duet) of the operating management and HR.

A rigorous discipline of planning and pursuit of talent excellence is weak or even absent in Indian companies, for the most part. Quite often, there exist no defined processes. Where there is a semblance of process, it tends to be personality-driven, rather than process-driven. It is worthwhile for corporates to work on this potential weak spot. Benchmarking processes against the best-in-class is a good way forward, just as management would do for total quality or productivity. Too often, the CEO leaves this complex task to Personnel/HR and deploys his personal energies on other important corporate issues.

The metaphor of parenting imaginatively highlights why excellence in talent management is among the toughest of corporate jobs. Both require a rigorous and sustained process discipline, soaked in a warm soup of empathy and emotion.

A few years ago, some faculty members of the SP Jain Institute of Management and Research and I conducted research on 'Shapers of Business Institutions'. One question asked of the CEOs and leaders was about how much of their time went into 'reflecting, thinking and planning of management talent'. The answers that we got ranged from 25 to 40 per cent. Those numbers are astonishingly high, but the answers offered a clue about how much top leaders value their own contribution to developing other leaders. An individual becomes a top leader with a principal responsibility to develop other leaders for the organisation.

I experienced how talent management was nurtured at Hindustan Unilever and tangentially witnessed this aspect in companies like Tata Consultancy, Tata Steel and Titan. I am certainly impressed by the care and time leaders and HR bestow upon nurturing and coaching talent within these companies. One measure of the success and capability is that, over several decades and successions, such companies can present more than one internal candidate to take over a vacancy without hesitation and without pause.

In parenting and leadership development, there is a need for rigorous process steeped in sensitivity and compassion. The processes must be as thorough as business and financial budgeting – with tight timelines, milestone markers, evaluations, discussions, challenges, innovation and calculated risk-taking. Execution is undoubtedly demanding. Just as the Chief Finance Officer (CFO) is the custodian of financial budgeting, the Chief Human Resources Officer (CHRO) should be the safekeeper of the talent-planning process. Talent planning and review should form an integral part of business planning. Too often in companies, these are two disconnected processes. Talent development demands intuitive considerations – the human element – at a much greater magnitude than working on budgets with numbers and figures. The cauldron is far more complex.

India is blessed to possess great leadership talent, but organisations must figure out how to cultivate and curate that talent.

Miyawaki mini forest for talent

When talent-building is discussed within organisations, the leaders often ask, 'Where does one start with such a long journey? How can we hit critical mass?' The anxiety is that their company is disadvantaged in not being as well established as a Unilever or Tata Steel. Their company does not have the luxury of taking talent processes for granted. It is a reasonable leadership concern.

Two vital life and career skills may unwittingly be learnt at the School of Hard Knocks – parenting a family and talent-building in an organisation. Just as securing a diploma in parenting does not assure parenting competence, corporate leaders (not just HR folks) learn the art of talent development by deep personal engagement, both emotionally and temporally.

The RIDE exercise – Recruitment, Induction, Development, Expansion – of human talent is both an infinite game and a complex task, not dissimilar to parenting. For a quick start at talent-building, leaders and HR may consider employing what I term the 'Miyawaki technique',[1] but with a health warning: Miyawaki may offer a quick start, but an evolutionary and biological process must follow it if the organisation wishes to develop long-term leadership talent.

In the 1960s, the Japanese botanist Professor Akira Miyawaki pioneered a technique of growing mini forests. Natural forests take several centuries to grow. They also require large land areas to develop. Inadequate land availability and urgent climate change–related pressures have both demanded some sort of quick start to ease the stress. So Miyawaki established a methodology to grow mini forests in small areas, faster – in mere decades, compared to centuries for regular forests. In an era of rapid urbanisation and concrete jungles, the Miyawaki technique delivers ecologically pleasing green cover in our endless, rolling urban spaces.

Mini forests, which are heavy in wood output, do not possess all the ecological advantages of natural forests. Mini forests are alright to get started, but obviously cannot replicate the benefits of natural forests. In the five walking spaces in front of my residence in Mumbai, I have seen shades of Miyawaki mini forests, though not quite the real thing. The lessons of Miyawaki mini forests can be considered for jump-starting a Miyawaki mini forest for talent! India Inc. may benefit from such an approach. But what might the Miyawaki technique look like when applied to talent?

According to Miyawaki, there are four categories of native plantings in any ecosystem – main tree species (tallest), sub-species (medium), shrubs (short), and ground-covering herbs – think of them as equivalent to top managers, technical and knowledge employees, skilled supervisors and less-skilled workmen in an organisation. About 50 to 100 local plant species belonging to these four categories are selected for planting, but in a dense manner – twenty to thirty times denser than what 'normal planting' would involve.

Here is an essential and important idea – the plants should be local and diverse and must be planted densely. This stage corresponds to what we call 'recruitment' in talent management. As successful talent development companies know, recruiting with density is the important first step for talent development. How much density? There is no rule. Allow for a 25–50 per cent attrition over five years – design recruitment density today, taking this into account. When I joined HUL as a trainee in 1967, the company recruited ten to fifteen trainees each year. Nowadays, they recruit at least six to seven times that number!

Next in talent management is induction. New recruits in any company should be hired for their positive attitude more than for ready skills. Skills can be taught, while attitude is difficult to cultivate. Fresh recruits are not aligned to the company's value system, ways of working, culture and relationships. Leadership must actively invest in these activities.

In Miyawaki mini forests, over the early years, after the soil has been mulched and prepared for porosity and permeability, the site is 'monitored, watered and weeded' to give the nascent forest a chance to establish itself. The densely spaced young plantings compete for light, water and nutrients. Such a struggle itself promotes rapid growth compared to traditional afforestation techniques. There exists a 'weeding-out' process in the mini forest, equivalent to attrition. Since attrition is inevitable, the denseness of talent recruitment assumes primacy. Trees in Miyawaki are known to grow about ten times faster than normal! Maybe quality talent, too, can be identified for survival and robustness early on. Recruits should be actively inducted into company values and goals by their line managers. Training courses, employee counselling by mentors, varied assignments, progress diaries – all of these and more are well-used techniques in good companies. In such a process, the less competent or uncommitted talent gets highlighted. Correction and, where necessary, weeding can then be done more effectively.

Miyawaki mini forests have the long-term limitation that they cannot replicate the benefits of natural forests. They provide quick and temporary green relief in concrete jungles. There is lots of wood available, but the many other benefits of a natural forest do not accrue. Likewise, developing a mini forest of talent provides a quick start and builds a positive talent atmosphere in a company. Thereafter, an organic and nurturing process, more like a biological process, is required within the company to develop that talent into long-term leadership talent.

The longer-term nurturing of talent is a large and a separate subject.

Is the Miyawaki technique of creating a mini forest of talent a 'proven concept'? Yes and no. Hindustan Unilever, Tata Steel, Infosys, Mahindra and the public sector behemoth National Thermal Power Corporation (NTPC), all have practised the art without terming their talent approach as such. If one studies their actions and approaches in talent building, one can trace the individual approaches to create a Miyawaki mini forest of talent.

CEO and Leadership Choices

When the CEO really matters

The reader can ponder over a philosophical question – when does the doctor matter most? If the patient is stable but suffering, the patient needs a very good general practitioner or surgeon. But if the patient is bleeding and urgent attention is required, the patient needs emergency medical aid. In both cases, the doctors and staff must be good, but in an emergency situation, they matter a lot more.

Similarly, the short answer to the transformation question is that the choice of the CEO matters a lot if the chosen leader is unfiltered. It matters less if the chosen leader is a product of fine filtration. The CEO selection matters in the relevant aspects, such as organisational transformation and institution building, both of which are driven by three imperatives: one, the pace of change in the company's industry; two, how urgent it is for the organisation to respond; and three, the choice of the leader who has to implement the transformation programme.

Does the company need urgent and major organisational change? If yes, how does the board identify the ideal leader to successfully supervise the transition? Does an individual leader matter at all, or is it the organisational momentum and history that determines the outcomes of any effort? Do circumstances create individual leaders or do individual leaders define their own circumstances? Answers to these questions define who is an unfiltered leader and who isn't.

I have read several books on leadership talent. George Anders explores how talent works in sports and how exceptional talent can make a dramatic difference; he also includes anecdotes on how coaches wagered successfully on a player despite contrarian indicators.[2] Christopher Clarey's biography of tennis star Roger Federer's career describes episodes when several talent spotters decided to back Federer despite doubts about whether he was a top-class exceptional player or not.[3]

However, for determining leadership in a company, how can a board decide who might make an exceptional leader? Professor Gautam Mukunda of HBS makes an enlightening contribution in the form of his book *Indispensable*,[4] the contents of which resonate with my own experiences. What does Professor Mukunda conclude from his research?

There are companies that practise a well-honed LFS or 'Leadership Filtration System'. For example, HUL has an explicit process to identify talent and groom managers to occupy future roles of leadership. Thus it is no wonder that HUL churns out leaders so frequently. Its system filters out the oddball, the seemingly eccentric manager. After a fruitful service record in the organisation, candidates for the top job emerge.

Filtered leaders tend to resemble each other. Obviously, they are not identical, even though they have passed through the same filters. Recall how in 1981, Reginald Jones, GE Chairman, selected his successor, Jack Welch. Or in 2002, when Jack Welch set up a process to select Jeff Immelt from among internal candidates. From an external perspective, it could be argued that it really did not matter too much which of the internal candidates was selected because they all had the potential to be equally successful CEOs.

Similarly, in HUL, from an outsider's perspective, Prakash Tandon was selected in preference to other candidates. Many years later, Ashok Ganguly was chosen over other candidates. There obviously must have been good reasons for these selections. But to be fair, there is no way to definitively say if any of the other aspirants could not have done a similarly terrific job. In short, LFS candidates, according to Professor Mukunda, tend to be interchangeable. They represent the median of the talent pool in a company, where the median is quite rich because of the efficiency of the filtration system.

The HUL pattern, though, is an exception in corporate India. Indeed, even in HUL, Chairman T. Thomas could be considered a mild variant of an unfiltered leader because for a few years in between he had left to join his family business. When Thomas was recruited back into HUL perhaps it was because he was a lateral thinker with different ideas. The condition of HUL at the time of his selection as chairman was life-threatening – a major portion of the company portfolio was under severe price controls; the government wanted to reduce foreign shareholding to 40 per cent or less; worker unions were militant. Such circumstances made it imperative to identify a leader with unconventional ideas, which Thomas was. He turned out to be a very successful CEO. Similarly, in the year 2005, the Unilever global board desired a dramatic change in the global organisation's unwieldy structure. For the first time, they recruited an external CEO, Paul Polman, who turned out to be quite a success.

At Tata, talent management was within the domain of individual Tata companies. Tata Steel, Tata Consultancy and Titan have a well-developed talent filtration system; for many decades, managers have advanced from among those who passed through the internal filtration system. Long-time insiders would, as a result, become potential candidates for the top job, and finally, one would be selected from among very close competitors. This was not so when it came to the group. Group leaders rarely changed. When J.R.D. Tata appointed his successor in 1991 after fifty-two years of chairmanship, Ratan Tata became the fifth chairman of the group in 120 years. There was no rigorous system of internal talent filtration at the group level and changes in group leadership were rare. Almost every appointment would be an unfiltered leader, including JRD himself in 1939, followed by Minoo Mody in the 1970s, who was appointed CEO of Tata Sons from A.F. Ferguson & Co.

I am sure that when I was appointed in 1998 as an executive director of Tata Sons, I was perceived as an unfiltered leader, while Ishaat Hussain must have been seen as a filtered executive director. Ratan Tata's successor, Cyrus Mistry, was also an unfiltered leader within the Tata group, though that succession did not end well. Chandra, former finance director of Tata Steel, later Tata Sons, is far more a product of the intensive TCS LFS.

It is helpful to explore whether any rules can be set for effective CEO selection. These rules may be applied and tested in other private sector companies, PSUs, family businesses and even in political institutions.

Successful unfiltered CEOs

To recapitulate, filtered CEOs are those who have been through graded sieves of organisational development within that company. For example, while I was a filtered leader in HUL, I wasn't one in Tata. Efficient filtration enables the production of a strong suite of internal leaders for the future. Apart from HUL's successful talent filtration system, other examples worthy of mention here are State Bank of India and HDFC Bank in financial services, McKinsey in consulting, and TCS and Infosys in software. Senior positions in competitor companies are often held by the alumni of such companies. On the other hand, unfiltered CEOs are recruits from outside the company. Both filtered and unfiltered leaders have their own value, depending on the circumstances of their recruitment. I shall explore some factors for the success of an unfiltered CEO.

The first factor requires the board to establish whether or not an industry is in the throes of turbulent change, or if the company is in crisis. The second factor is creating adequate distance between the incumbent CEO and the new appointee – this is vital because an unfiltered leader is considered a recruitment risk compared to a filtered leader. They could turn out to be 'extreme' – either greatly successful or greatly unsuccessful.

Lou Gerstner's appointment at IBM was an example of the success of an unfiltered leader. In 1992, John Akers, a thirty-year veteran at IBM, had been CEO and Chairman before Gerstner. IBM was going through a crisis of sales, profits and cash flow. The board decided to bring in an outsider, an unfiltered leader. Lou Gerstner had an MBA from Harvard and was an alumnus of McKinsey and RJR Nabisco, and was sought out. Gerstner initially regretted that he was neither a technology whiz, nor thought it possible to save the rapidly declining IBM. But the headhunter persisted with the additional blandishment that President Bill Clinton would call to persuade him because it was he who wished to save the iconic American enterprise. Gerstner finally relented and joined IBM, but John Akers made a clean exit from the company thereafter. The story of how IBM was saved is captured masterfully in Gerstner's *Who Says Elephants Can't Dance?*, which I would highly recommend you read.

Now consider the unhappy stories of Ramesh Sarin of Voltas and Chris Viehbacher of Sanofi. I have elaborated on the facts in great detail in my 2019 book, *Crash*.[5] Here is a brief summary. Voltas was an unwieldy Tata company. For many years, the CEO was A.H. Tobaccowala, who ran the company with a firm hand, based on rules and procedures. However, the company was not in a turbulent technology area nor was it faced with an existential crisis like IBM. Nonetheless, the board decided to recruit 'the best leader in the world', an unfiltered leader.

Ramesh Sarin had been a filtered leader at ITC for several years. His strength was that he was a customer-focused manager. After Sarin occupied the corner office at Voltas, he found the shadow of Tobaccowala everywhere because he had not made a clean exit. He chaired board meetings as non-executive chairman and leveraged his long-standing connections within the company to keep abreast of the goings-on. Sarin's strategy to transform Voltas from a rules-based company into a customer-focused company was met with several obstacles. Sarin left the company before his five-year term expired.

Sanofi is an archetypal French pharma company, formed through several M&As. Jean-François Dehecq became CEO in 2004, followed by a research leader, Dr Gérard Le Fur, who only had a short tenure. By September 2008, the Sanofi board had decided to look outside. The pharma industry was becoming increasingly global. The company was not in crisis, though its performance was sluggish. The board decided to recruit Chris Viehbacher, a German-Canadian pharma veteran with twenty years' experience, a superb track record and reputation, from

GlaxoSmithKline. In line with the mandate that he believed he had, along with his business instincts, Viehbacher implemented an agenda of global acquisitions and hired several international managers. Over the next six years, the company made acquisitions worth US$30 billion. Obviously, his management style was way different from the group of directors, who were a strong French influence. After six years, the directors thought it best to part ways with Viehbacher. Chairman Serge Weinberg temporarily ran the company till they recruited Olivier Brandicourt, a French business leader, who had served in Bayer Healthcare and Pfizer.

From these and other examples, it could be hypothesised that the success of an unfiltered leader depends largely on five conditions:

1. The company's industry is in churn or turmoil.
2. The company requires speedy internal reorientation.
3. There is no suitable leader within the organisation.
4. The CEO mandate is shaped to fit the strength of a particular chosen candidate and the boundaries within which the CEO is to perform are agreed upon. Ideally, the outgoing CEO should make a clean break with the company.
5. The unfiltered leader has not been chosen because they are the best but because they fit the company's needs best. This is an important distinction to make.

In hindsight, had these criteria been explicit at the time of recruitment, the outcomes of the failed scenarios may also have been different. Many allied questions may arise, but they are fuel for future writings.

Summary

- It is essential to build a strong suite of leaders and managers in a company.

- Talent density at the lower levels is an important requirement to be acted upon.
- The choice of the CEO and leadership team is crucial. If the company is in an 'emergency situation', an unfiltered leader might be considered a worthwhile risk.
- If the company is not in an emergency situation, a filtered leader may be a more worthwhile choice.

5

Review

Checks and Balances

It is natural for a leader to consider several aspects at the time their company's transformation programme is being finalised. Some focus on the 'what to do' category and others on the 'how to do' category. From the 'how to do' category, two vectors have been considered in this chapter:
- How will the leader know how things are going?
- How will the leader know what to correct and when?

Is Your Transformation Programme Working?

Organisational transformation will disturb the status quo and help to build business institutions. Change efforts are akin to raising a family, as I have mentioned before. The parents are never quite certain whether things are working the way they had planned. Their work appears to be permanently in progress. Whether in a company or a country, this is true from an inside as well as outside perspective. There is no way to be sure of the outcomes of the effort because one is not dealing with logical inputs with predictable outputs, but with human responses to inputs with unpredictable outcomes.

Imagine you are the shareholder of a long-standing company. For about seven years, a charismatic CEO and his leadership team have been implementing their transformation programme, exuding confidence, panache and bravado, bordering on arrogance. The earlier leaders came from either a family-managed company or a multinational corporation. The current team prides itself on being culturally home-grown and thoroughly professional. Absence of Western or family influence is touted as an asset, further embellished with gorgeous, national sartorial displays instead of Western business suits.

After the passage of several years, despite high-decibel declarations about the company's performance, the company's results are not as glamorous or appealing as the leadership team would like investors to believe. Doubts start rising about whether the new culture being embedded is proving to be toxic and damaging the traditional values of the reputed company. Shareholders begin feeling concerned about the leadership.

What are the ominous signals and symptoms that would reveal whether an undesirable toxicity is at play in the organization in such a case? Here is an example to illustrate how this might be achieved in place of a table of checklist points.

The current leadership team belongs to a particular school of thought and is biased towards a certain style of management. Culturally, their way of thinking and behaving is different from the Western MNC or traditional family businesses. Their way tends to produce similar-thinking alumni with a shared management ideology. The leader's charismatic and magnetic personality are perforce unifying points for those working in the company. While explaining the results, the leader and his team might adopt unusual but recognisable ways that shareholders must look out for:

(i) Leaders blame predecessors for every malaise

For seven years, predecessors have been regular punching bags for the top team: 'if only the predecessor had not left the company in such a weak and fragile condition'; 'if only the predecessors had invested more in human capital and training'; 'if only they had been more decisive while dealing with difficult situations'; 'if only the predecessors had not been so docile while confronting domestic and global competition'; 'if only the predecessors had adopted a more company-centric strategy'.

The list is endless – if all or at least most problems could have been resolved earlier, the company would hardly have been atoning for the multiple, grievous errors of the past. It would be in a much stronger position on almost all fronts today.

(ii) The new leaders make tall promises, yet there are doubts about delivery

They might offer cogent reasons for repeatedly and continuously missing targets. According to the contemporary leadership, the leaders' senior operating colleagues are in stasis, acting with an outmoded mindset; accounts and data of the past several years need correction and restatement to mirror the current positive profit performance more accurately; competitors are hitting below the belt with unsavoury moves never witnessed before. Domestic media revels in negative reportage with no analysis on the positive actions taken and in place; there are no admirers of this fast-progressing and immensely successful company in foreign press, hence they are getting hammered in overseas coverage. The fantastic results being achieved all the time are ignored. There is a ceaseless assault from once-in-a-century disasters caused by the global economy.

(iii) The top team is articulate, yet belligerent and pugnacious

They are excellent communicators and speakers. Being alumni from the same school of thought, they are all built in a vituperative mould. The chiefs of finance, administration, human resources, public relations speak in a harsh, combative manner. They defend themselves by attacking past leaders! They brook little criticism. Even their media spokespersons defend the company by viciously attacking competitors.

(iv) Shareholders and the public cannot comprehend the leadership's 'brilliant, newfangled' ideas

The company periodically announces dramatic schemes to benefit stakeholders and owners. But after months of debate and protestations played out in corporate courts and media, the leadership is compelled to withdraw several proposals. Based on the leaders' logic, the forward-thinking proposals and actions to benefit shareholders were not understood within the proper context. The culprits: misinformation campaigns by competitors and a hostile media.

(v) Days of wine and roses are ahead, though the better future takes time

When the current leaders were selected seven years ago, they assured the company would soon be entering a golden future. After five years, they desired the board and shareholders to renew their employment contract. They expressed confidence that magical times await the company in the next five years or even sooner. Now it appears that more than a decade is required for the change to manifest itself. The new corporate leaders proclaim that days of wine and roses are just one or two bends away!

If you were a shareholder of this company, how would you view their transformation efforts? Is the leadership acting with empathy and sensitivity for the employees? Do such leaders evoke trust? Above all, do you regard them as self-obsessed and a harmful bunch and vote for change, even though a new uncertainty would surely arise with a different and unknown leadership?

Readers will recognise these symptoms by recalling the state of public discourse and politics in several societies. Think of Germany and Italy under Adolf Hitler and Benito Mussolini. Coming to contemporary times, think of Britain, Brazil, Turkey and our South Asian region. All of these symptoms are visible and clear.

Protect the Corporation through Immunisation

Engaged employees provide the best immunity to a corporation, as long-life companies like Mahindra, Godrej, Bajaj, Unilever and Tata have demonstrated. I shall explore the metaphor of the human immune system and the corporate body in my attempt to further illustrate this theory.

Vaccination protects a human being from invisible diseases. Corporations also suffer the ravages of invisible diseases arising from adequate people power and employee negativity. If you had access to the right vaccine, it might be possible to strengthen corporate immunity. Corporate crises demonstrate that, like humans, organisations too need to guard against invisible attacks. We cannot ensure thriving human or organisational health by ignoring invisible attackers. In my view, a very effective vaccine would be required to neutralise an invisible attack on companies, which can be termed as 'People Shield', which deploys people power to fight against infection from invisible attackers.

Reflective executives should plan their future agenda. The focus on unleashing people's power can appear to be a soft remedy for a rather serious threat, centred around passion, culture and positivity. But people power can make a company resilient against any kind of attacks on its constitution. A company is prone to virus-like attacks such as employee disengagement, inconsistent leadership behaviour, festering grievances, and negativity at the workplace. For too many years, managers have been emphasising efficiency at the expense of humanity and empathy.

I studied the writings of Professor Michael Watkins, an immunologist-turned-management academic, and was deeply inspired.[1] The human immune system is an active communication network comprised of a complex set of cells, antibodies and signalling mechanisms. These elements are arranged in three layers: the outermost physical layer (skin and mucous membranes); the second is the innate layer, which is the protective layer of cells that we are born with; finally, there is the adaptive layer, which refers to the mechanisms that recognise and respond to an attack.

What are the equivalents for a company? Corporate immunity is provided by engaged and responsive people in the company, arranged in three layers:
1. the physical layer, people's visible passion
2. the innate layer, the organisational culture
3. the adaptive layer, positivity exceeding negativity.

The physical layer: Visible passion

A highly engaged workforce acts as the physical layer of company immunology. Engaged employees care for the company deeply, recommend the company to non-employees, work collaboratively and emotionally guard the company against unwelcome attackers. I have tracked the published data and find that employee engagement data for the past decade and a half shows that employee engagement has steadily declined in most companies everywhere. This is an unfavourable trend.

As an example of engaged employees in action, recall the fabulous response of the Taj Hotel employees during the terrorist attack of 26/11. Employees at all levels went well beyond job descriptions and assigned duties to protect their customers. Several valiant employees lost their lives in the process. Their behaviour symbolised an unrehearsed practice of the adage '*athithi devo bhava*'.

The innate layer: Culture

The human immune system works by recognising what is of 'self' and 'non-self', and by maintaining an equilibrium between overreaction and underreaction. Every organisation has a political system and culture, which defines what is perceived as its 'self'. Culture acts as the innate layer of the immune system and prevents destructive thinking from invading the company atmosphere.

Every company has an articulated or implicit corporate purpose, which is the basis for the employees' concept of 'self'.

For example, in normal times, technologists and infrastructure-oriented managers scoff at the modest job of consumer marketers and makers of soap or toilet cleaners. During COVID-19 times, employees in Unilever got a sense of renewed purpose, just as hospitals and medical professionals did.

The adaptive layer: Positivity

Psychology professor Barbara Fredrickson is a thought leader in positive psychology. She has developed a technique to measure positivity and negativity at the workplace.[2] According to her, when the ratio of positivity to negativity exceeds 3, then employees are positive and build a resilience to adversity. According to her, 80 per cent of American employees are at less than 3 – I cannot help but wonder about Indian employees. In my experience, when leaders visibly practise good listening and empathy, positivity increases.

Humans fight invasive threats through an adaptive mechanism, the brain and the senses being analogous to top leadership and the far ends of the organization, respectively. The signals of external attack are first sensed at the periphery, that is, by front-line salesmen and factory workers. Organisations must sharpen their listening and response mechanisms; they must welcome diverse expert opinions. That is how management can secure employee engagement and positivity, just as the World Health Organization (WHO) recommended proactive community involvement as the most important response to COVID-19 during the 2020 global pandemic.

Managers of the future should reflect on how to administer jabs of People Shield to their employees and ecosystem – encouraging visible passion, purposeful culture and positivity. Together, they unleash the power of the people, which is the best immunisation for a company. It is worthwhile for managers and agents of change in all realms to reflect on what they can do about this. Leaving it to the top leadership alone would be a mistake.

Summary

- The execution of organisational transformation is greatly helped if the company has engaged employees.
- As the leadership executes the transformation plan, there is the inevitable need to review and correct course.
- Transformers may suffer from the tendency to overpromise so that the 'drama' of transformation is heightened. It is dangerous to do so. It is always better to under-promise and over-deliver and one should be wary in the case of the opposite.

6

Long Life

Continual Renewal

Just as it is for human beings, mortality is certain for companies, too. Human beings are advised to lead whatever life they have with good health and cheer. Companies too must strive for the same. Why is it then that some companies survive and grow for a century or more, while others die sooner or get taken over? What is the secret for a long and adaptive life for companies?

The Brahma Mantra for Long-life Companies

Transformation on a continual basis is essential for maintaining corporate youthfulness and agility. What do history and anthropology tell us about long-life companies? Is there an equivalent of Ayurveda or ikigai for companies, a secret sauce for a long-life company?

I have had the fortune of working with two companies, both over a hundred years old and growing stronger, Unilever and Tata. Over the past five decades of close association with these exceptional companies, I have gathered some experiences and observations on what keeps them youthful. Their attitude and practices are based on the art of youthfulness. I have also been inspired by several well-researched and relevant books that have studied different kinds of companies – from family-managed Japanese companies to American public companies. The observations and lessons alluded to in these books converge to comprise a set of common principles. I derive comfort from the fact that the lessons I have drawn from my experiences resonate with these principles.

Drawing from traditional Indian wisdom, we learn about four principles for a long and fulfilling life: know yourself; protect nature; serve others; be firm but act with compassion. This vedantic formula also works for companies. A corporation does not work or exist in isolation. It is a part of an ecosystem. Its very existence and fate are linked with those of its stakeholders. It has a much larger role to play for the community than is commonly understood and practised. Lots of research, case studies and consulting assignments on corporate success or failure have focused on what the organisation does, rather than what the organisation is part of.

Applying the nature principle, an organisation must be viewed as part of a bigger ecosystem, in line with the most fundamental law of nature: in order to survive, a species must adapt to its environment. The '212 principle' states that water at 211 degrees Fahrenheit is still water, but one degree more and it will convert into steam. Employees within organisations need to have just that little extra stretch in their efforts to propel the organisation forward.

I summarise five key features of long-life companies as I have gathered from my experiences and published literature, as follows:

(i) Living for a consistently sought purpose

Creating a purpose statement and living to achieve it consistently through actions and behaviours ensures that over time, it is deeply ingrained and becomes a part of life for all stakeholders, especially employees. The purpose does not change over long periods of time, although the expression may be revised and modernised periodically. In the purpose statement of Tata, for example, four strands stand out: (i) improving the quality of life of communities; (ii) leadership in sectors of national economic significance; (iii) returning to society what is earned; (iv) formalising high standards of behaviour.

(ii) Organising to deliver a long-term vision

Tata was a textile company in the beginning, whereas these days, it is viewed as a software and digital technology company. The metamorphosis has been continual, for over a century. The Tata group's growth over the years is a fitting tribute to the robust business model that it adopts, and which has found favour with all its stakeholders. The group creates, develops and nurtures businesses of national significance. It ensures that any business that it enters into will impact all the stakeholders positively – most importantly, society at large – and contribute to nation-building. The group believes in value creation in a manner whereby short-term gains can and are often sacrificed if they are in conflict with the value system that defines the group. Creating and living a holistic purpose also instils a focus that encourages employees to shun short-term opportunistic behaviour.

(iii) Creating an adaptive, collaborative and tolerant ecosystem

As opposed to a classical organisation structure, derived from principles of physics, Tata derives inspiration from the principles of botany to make their ecosystem more permeable. Instead of rigid boundaries, this permeability allows easy exchange of views and ideas, leading to a collaborative effort. Apart from some boundary conditions that are central to the group's purpose, this structure gives full autonomy to the group companies to experiment and innovate. Tata is a rare case of the holding company being private, while the operating companies are public. Such a species is rare in the world!

(iv) Living in harmony with nature

The group has always been focused on living in harmony with nature. For instance, Tata Power has an aggressive target to source a substantial share of power from renewable sources. Dedicated sustainability cells in the company continually monitor and reduce the negative impact of the company's activities on people and the environment. In fact, many companies proactively have started generating meaningful products from effluents. The carbon footprint of the fifty largest Tata companies has been estimated and their carbon management strategy articulated accordingly. The remaining smaller Tata companies are still being mapped. Early estimates indicate that specific emissions can be brought down by 10–15 per cent if Tata companies adopt abatement measures, instead of going down the business-as-usual growth path.

Thus, while the journey began with the intention of doing the right thing as a socially responsible corporate house, it may well turn out that this has been the right thing to do from a business perspective as well.

(v) Being conservative with financing

Just like humans need to be careful about their health, what they eat, how much they exercise, etc., a healthy dose of conservatism improves longevity of companies. In *The Living Company*, Arie de Geus says, 'Such companies are frugal and do not risk their capital gratuitously. They understand the meaning of money in an old-fashioned way and know the usefulness of spare cash in the kitty.'[1] Tata surely subscribes to this view and is not perceived as one of those swashbuckling and aggressive corporations that want to grow at any cost.

Corporate Ayurveda for Rejuvenating Companies

Organisational transformation is like rejuvenating the human body and mind. The pursuit of life and career imposes stresses on managers, just as nurturing of start-ups does on founding teams. In the bloom of adolescence and youth, every person inadvertently subjects the human body to enormous stresses through unhealthy habits, lifestyle and bravado. Rejuvenation involves going to the yoga centre, naturopathy clinic or weight-loss camp and rediscovering new perspectives on old matters, for example, breathing techniques. The rejuvenation efforts for transforming organisations are the equivalent of yoga for the body – what one may term as 'corporate Ayurveda'.

Leaders must adopt a regime of corporate Ayurveda. The need first manifests when the company misses on a few health parameters, enters a phase of steady decline, or suffers an enterprise 'heart attack'. Advancing the metaphor, one could view the process as the equivalent of resetting habits and diet, strengthening the core muscles of the body, and keeping the mind active and engaged.

This requires an understanding of what patterns of action and mindset a long-life company encourages. One essential aspect for the company, as with human beings, is to adopt a *satvik* and responsible lifestyle. There has been a resurgence of interest among management scholars around the subject of sustainable, honest and enlightened business practices in terms of societal matters. What is responsible business and what is the role of business in society? History offers both examples and lessons.

Two hundred years ago, the Neanderthal version of the modern enterprise adopted two remarkable innovations: double-entry accounting and the joint stock company. These two innovations permitted entrepreneurs to think big even with limited capital – the joint stock company limited owners' liabilities to their share capital and thus facilitated taking greater risks, which is, of course, at the heart of enterprise. The accounting innovation required every transaction to be recorded in two aspects: debit and credit, corresponding to the person giving the benefit and the person receiving the benefit.

Thus a long-prevailing entrepreneurial mindset adapted and evolved into an industrial mindset. With the advent of the Industrial Revolution, industry could earn disproportionate wealth for the shareholder, which included the founder. Traders too earned money, but never on the scale that industrialists could.

Examples of such entrepreneurs are the founders of both the corporates where I had the privilege of working – Unilever and Tata.

By the 1880s, William Hesketh Lever had amassed a fortune by launching his Sunlight and Lifebuoy soap empire. Lord Leverhulme, as he became known by the time he died, left his fortune in a Leverhulme Trust with a mandated social purpose. In a striking parallel, Jamsetji Tata began his enterprise in textiles around the same time. Investing in risk-taking by acquiring sick textile mills, deploying the latest techniques of production on looms and weaving, producing textiles more productively than their competitors, namely, Lancashire, Jamsetji became wealthy. Jamsetji and his successors also left their wealth in trusts to engage with social issues.

Both Lever and Tata were probably influenced by the contemporary philosophical thinking prevalent in the world's prosperous nations. Influenced by the thinking of the English philosopher Jeremy Bentham, British capitalism had several benign features. Entrepreneurship in America developed sharply in contrast and led to the emergence of what history has come to refer to as the 'robber barons'. Rockefeller, Carnegie, Ford, John Pierpont Morgan, for example, were initially controversial, but left their wealth in foundations for the service of the community. These foundations do a great deal for social and economic upliftment of weaker sections to this day.

Influenced also by prevalent ideas of the late 1800s, the initial corporations seemed to develop an ethical and socially oriented outlook. Initially, it took entrepreneurs time to shake off trading conservatism in decision-making. Attitudes morphed as entrepreneurs turned to manufacturing, which employs large labour forces. When a big opportunity shows up unanticipated, as with the Californian Gold Rush and sea voyaging for new lands, some entrepreneurs get carried away – as the current surge in the start-up economy also indicates. Innovation, creativity and ambition abounded, as did cowboy mentalities, greater risk-taking and an increased mortality among enterprises. In the drive for survival and growth, enterprises focused more on rational and technological aspects – labour productivity, new manufacturing techniques, capital efficiency – and on squeezing out more and more from less and less.

What a Business Institution Is

Readers may feel that while there is much to learn from centurions, what about more contemporary companies? I explore two questions in a more contemporary context by reviewing the journeys of some companies born around the time of India's economic liberalisation:
- What is a 'business institution'?
- What is the mindset, behaviour and action of the 'shaper' of a business institution?

Start-ups can develop a mindset of business institution-building early on. It is helpful to consider the Shapers' MBA – Mindset, Behaviour and Action. I define 'institution' as an organisation that has, at its core, at least three characteristics: first, it has high values and norms for which it is greatly admired; second, it has withstood pressures of finance, business and regulation, and thus has developed an innate resilience; third, its economic and stakeholder returns in comparison with those of its peers are at the upper end, though not necessarily the best. To define the Shapers' MBA grid, we create an 8x3 matrix. The three vertical columns are Mindset, Behaviour and Actions. The eight horizontal rows represent dimensions based on Purpose, People, Policies and Processes. The eight dimensions are – three essential ones, highlighted in bold, and five optional:

i. **People Relations**
ii. **Short-term and Long-term Focus**
iii. **Critical Thinking**
iv. Orbit Shifting
v. Breaking Barriers
vi. Levers of Change
vii. Cyclical Learning
viii. Stakeholder Orientation

Mindset	Behaviour	Action
People relations: Respectful to others	Sensitive and empathetic to others	Engages with people and nurtures them
Short term versus long term: Both are equally important	Encourages to deal with the immediate while silently considering the long term	Acts on the immediate decisively to get results, creating the impression of small wins so as to look forward to and work towards a 'big' victory in the future
Critical thinking: Considers options and their pros and cons in mental evaluation	Encourages discussion and debate with open-mindedness	Acts with precision and demands accountability
Orbit changing: Constant evaluation of which orbit change will benefit the organisation	Tosses around and debates the risks and rewards of orbit change, almost appearing indecisive	Demonstrates single-minded commitment once a decision is made
Breaking barriers: I have the freedom to act if I am willing to steer through obstacles	Identifies the obstacles and seeks the best way to deal with them—break them, go around them, navigate them	Once the path is clear, pursues with an Arjuna-like determination
Levers of change: Action is within my reach—must change complacency to the aspirational mindset	Debates and seeks ways to dislodge the organisation from negative hooks while attaching positive hooks	Presses for action and change in a disciplined manner
Cyclical learning: Action Observation Benchmark Review—Act again	Insists on a systems approach of cyclical learning	Ensures organisation-wide deployment of an accepted system
Stakeholder orientation: What is good for the stakeholder is good for the institution and hence for us	Constantly understanding customer and community perspective	Always acts keeping in mind multiple stakeholder interests

Source: Extracted from *How TCS Built an Industry for India*, R. Gopalakrishnan and Tulsi Jayakumar, Rupa, 2019.

TCS was established in 1968 in a nation which suffered from scarcity of food, electricity and infrastructure. TCS can be described as a 'black swan' event, characterised by rarity, extreme impact and retrospective predictability. Faqir Chand Kohli, the effective founder, had the shaper's technical knowledge, but also a knack for spotting gaps. Kohli could iteratively shape the environment as well as the organisation. The initial TCS plan was to import computers and serve Indian companies by deploying electronic data processing. In a milieu wherein the public sector Life Insurance Corporation of India (LIC) could not even open the boxes in which it had imported its first ICL 1903 computer, and an economy which was desperately short on foreign exchange, TCS pivoted by seeking customers outside India to drive its business. That is how they invented the India offshoring model.

By 1996, when Kohli handed over the executive role of CEO to his protégé, S. Ramadorai, TCS was deriving over 90 per cent of its revenue from overseas, employing 8,000 people and had reached a revenue of US$160 million per year. It had engineered profitability into its DNA through frugality and customer value focus. Its shareholder Tata Sons was not enthusiastic to infuse dollops of cash to support losses, if incurred, as venture funds do nowadays. Between 1996 and 2009, the Ramadorai years, TCS multiplied its revenue and employee strength many times over by riding the Y2K wave, converting software development into having factory-like efficiency and precision, and raising customer service to global standards. The TCS IPO happened as late as 2004 at a starting valuation of US$2 billion. Today, thanks to its frugality and efficiency, TCS enjoys a market capitalisation of over US$120 billion and employs over half a million associates without the fuss of ever having been called a unicorn!

Philosopher Thomas Kuhn argued that scientific breakthroughs happen when a researcher observes the world well enough to identify and explain an anomaly. The discovery of an anomaly, a surprise, gives scientists the opportunity to revisit a theory to better understand it. This often leads to a modification or improvement of the existing theory to accommodate or offer reasons for the existence of the anomaly.

Like we instil certain things from childhood, start-ups must consider doing the right things from the beginning, too.

i. The first essential is 'people relations'. This refers to the shapers' obsession to engage with people, constantly nurturing their skills/expertise. Shapers tend to accord this higher priority than business planning. For example, as described in one book, A.M. Naik's seven-step leadership process.[2]

ii. 'Short term and long term' refer to a counterintuitive mindset – to spend clock time to robustly solve short-term problems, without reducing the emotional time to think through the long-term issues. A mother raising her child exemplifies this ability. Kiran Mazumdar-Shaw maintained a laser-sharp focus on solid-state fermentation, while thinking through the benefits of an alternative technology for a biopharma entry by Biocon.

iii. 'Critical thinking' refers to the ability to generate new options in decision-making: the obvious ones strike most managers anyway. For example, TCS's creation of software tools to automate software development to effectively exploit the explosive Y2K opportunity.

Biocon is interesting because it has been founded and nurtured by a woman entrepreneur in the biotech field – one that tends to be male-dominated – especially when she entered the fermentation industry in 1978. Imagine a Gujarati-origin, Kannada-speaking, Australian-trained female brew master, seeking a job back in India! Her Australian classmate recommended her name for an Indian entrepreneur partner for an upcoming Irish fermentation company called Biocon. She met the company with a dream, but faced understandable scepticism. That is why Kiran calls herself an 'accidental entrepreneur'; perhaps all entrepreneurs are accidental, in that sense.

How did a group of Biocon companies get conceived, all sharing a common parentage, but operating as a federation of independent companies? How did the Indian progeny of the

Irish Biocon then end up buying the parent company in Ireland? How did this disruptor company become profitable early enough to parent other companies thereafter? How did this company, founded on the robust, *koji* solid-state fermentation technology, pivot towards the delicate biopharma technology in an India which had no high-skilled professionals in the field of biological sciences and manufacturing control systems?

These days, the Biocon group ranks among the global top twenty-five biosciences companies. It debuted in an IPO as late as 2004 at a valuation of US$1 billion, and fifteen years later, has aggregated a market capitalisation worth six times more. The company is about to enter the US market with its biosimilar insulin in partnership with Mylan, Inc., but in the process, it will also sell a diabetes treatment that will cost consumers about 10 per cent of what the current treatments cost – exporting C.K. Prahalad's bottom-of-the-pyramid idea to America.[3] Once written down prosaically, the 'Biocon Way' may sound obvious, but Prahalad's book provides deep management insights into the grammar that underlies that prose. The compass of Biocon leadership has six traits:

- Confident humility
- Critical thinking
- Focus on challenges, not tasks
- Experimental mindset
- Employee engagement through freedom to operate
- Conservative financing

Biocon is an institution in the making. The shaper's influence imparts to the group a great chance of successfully overcoming future vicissitudes.

Shaping the Institution

A good company is run by a competent CEO, but a business institution is crafted by a shaper. A company that makes India proud is briefly described below: Larsen & Toubro (L&T).

Former Managing Director K. Venkataramani reflected on L&T's orbit-changing strategies (he credits A.M. Naik) by saying, 'What is today's L&T is because we could move from simple fabrication to nuclear, space, defence, oil and gas. Our construction wing moved from simple road construction to complex construction projects like airports and metros.'

While effecting this transformation, then CEO Anil Naik demanded 'critical thinking' from the leadership team to uncover why L&T was valued poorly compared to blue chip companies. In 1999, when Naik assumed leadership, L&T was valued at INR 5,000 crore. Given the complexity and scale of its projects, he wondered why it was not INR 2,50,000 crore. This required the team to identify the levers of change available. Naik was willing to admit that he did not really understand the science and art of share pricing.

He led Project Blue Chip, which deconstructed the logic of share pricing as a result that reflects the value created by the company. Disassembling the formula for share pricing into its parts brought into full view what levers the management had for positively and constructively influencing the market perception. Such understanding would not leave pricing purely to the whim of the share market.

When the ownership of L&T seemed vulnerable, Naik's critical thinking led to an unusual insight. He saw a distinction between financial ownership and emotional ownership. It struck him like a bolt from the blue that L&T was emotionally owned by workers, though this was not the case from a financial point of view. This changed his mindset, which in turn triggered change in behaviours and actions to solve the short-term problem using a long-term perspective. The cement business was sold, an L&T Employees' Welfare Trust was set up, employees were given stocks of the company and Naik made his most enduring contribution as a shaper when he aligned the financial ownership with the emotional ownership of the company.

Switching to TCS, consider what S. Ramadorai did when he was confronted with an unknown called Y2K. He reckoned that it was both a hardware and a software problem. Based on the customised software developed over the years, TCS had several migration tools in its repertoire. Y2K was essentially a mainframe computer problem, so TCS established a 'software factory' in Chennai to handle 650 million lines of code. This smart move, arising out of a critical thinking approach, resulted in a sharp revenue increase from US$125 million in 1995 to US$419 million within four years!

Apart from critical thinking and orbit-changing approaches, another similarity between the shaping of TCS and L&T concerned the shapers' approach to human resources and talent development. Fascinating narratives emerged in our interviews about how the shapers pored over talent files, connected directly with talent and took risks with young and upcoming leaders. It is then hardly surprising that both TCS and L&T found successors who were fifteen to twenty years younger than Ramadorai and Naik, respectively, at the time of their handing over the baton of CEO.

Of, by and for the People

After the American Civil War in the 1860s, Abraham Lincoln delivered a brief but historic speech. He invoked 'a government of the people, by the people, for the people' in his famous Gettysburg address, and spelled out indelibly the core element of any institution: people.

Corporations also benefit by adopting the same unfaltering truth: people orientation is at the core of business institutions, just as in democratic nations. Companies of, by and for the people become institutions. Shapers are known for exceptionally high people-oriented mindsets, inter alia, and thus contribute to society and communities, while also incidentally making profits.

Take the case of TCS. When there were less than ten database experts in Mumbai, TCS pioneered the creation of skilled human resources to seed a new industry for India. F.C. Kohli, the father of Indian IT, worked closely with Dr P.K. Kelkar, who oversaw development of the Indian Institutes of Technology (IITs), to develop the first MTech programme in computer science at IIT Kanpur. Kohli attracted talent from the Massachusetts Institute of Technology (MIT), University of California Los Angeles (UCLA) and Harvard. When S. Ramadorai took over, the Indian IT industry was growing at a scorching 40 per cent per year and the human resource challenge had acquired a different dimension altogether. Ram (as he is commonly known) and his team initiated 'Ignite', a programme to train non-engineering graduates to become business consultants who could travel the world and speak the one language of TCS. TCS has since managed to increase its employee strength forty times over twenty-three years, from 10,000 employees in 1996 to 4,17,000 in 2019, with the lowest attrition rate in the industry.

Building an organisation through hiring the right people by catching them young and in possession of the desired work ethic and values, and allowing them to explore their potential, has been the formula for success for the behemoth of India's financial sector, the HDFC group. As Deepak Parekh, the shaper of the HDFC group, said, 'We always say that we hire ordinary people and make them do extraordinary things.' What better way than this to epitomise Abe Lincoln's 'of the people'?

Marico's shaper Harsh Mariwala caught on early that an organisation could command human qualities like creativity, passion and initiative. What is necessary is to ensure that an institution is built 'by the people' who did not just have these three qualities but could also ensure that a work culture where people are encouraged to take risks without punishing failure was maintained. It also meant empowerment of a certain nature which had not been imagined hitherto in India Inc. Thus, Marico entrusts employees with maintaining their own attendance and leave records – with the HR department neither monitoring nor maintaining any such records themselves – reimbursements for expenses incurred at work are also self-administered, thus doing away with routine bureaucratic processes.

Such empowerment and encouragement of an entrepreneurial orientation is characteristic of other business institutions like Kotak Mahindra Bank (KMB) as well. However, to let the organisation be built by people, the shaper needs to be one to revel in helming a team of achievers, who have free rein to question, challenge and express dissent. Uday Kotak's team at KMB has had people like Shanti Ekambaram, who was a tough competitor for him in his early career days. As Uday says, 'If your team members are better than you, that's what you want.' Anil Naik of L&T is equally open to feedback from his employees, and has been known to often ask them a simple, direct question: 'What do you think we need to transform this company?'

While profits are the oxygen of business organisations, institutions exist primarily 'for the people'. Biocon is one such institution, with its shaper, not unsurprisingly, epitomising a business with courage and heart. Kiran Mazumdar-Shaw believes that she was following her heart by manufacturing and supplying insulin to the poor in the US. It was her courage which made her take on the big players in that market and profitably sell her brand of insulin at a fraction of the price: 90 per cent of the poor and immigrant population in the US use Biocon's insulin, which costs US$5 per unit, compared to US$200–250 per unit at which insulin is sold by the other large drug manufacturing companies.[4]

Keen business sense apart, almost all shapers and their business institutions have been associated with giving back to society. L&T's Naik remains deeply committed to the community and has pledged 75 per cent of his wealth to social causes. Marico gives back to society through mentoring and facilitating entrepreneurs to scale their ventures through the Marico Innovation Foundation, while the Kotak Education Foundation and support for a badminton academy managed by Pulella Gopichand are KMB's ways of discharging corporate social responsibility.

In conclusion, business institutions are known for the people they create, who in turn recreate them.

The Art of Critical Thinking

We have reviewed a great practice of institution builders, namely, their leveraging of people power. I now describe the second practice of institution building called 'critical thinking'. What is critical thinking? It is a capacity that contributes to organisational resilience and agility by compelling managements to challenge the existing reality and think up new ones. It has to do with developing unusual scenarios for problem-solving by thinking up not-so-obvious options. Leaders think critically by reflecting on the *context of an issue* rather than simply analysing the facts of an issue. Consider this example of how Biocon pivoted its technology.

After ten years of Biocon's existence, Kiran Mazumdar-Shaw reflected on its growth options. The company had begun with a conventional technology (called solid state), which was suitable in the light of local conditions, such as water and power availability. An alternative was sophisticated tech called deep tank.

Biocon's leadership team was faced with a choice one decade into their inception: should the company be content with being a big fish in a small pond (solid state), or should they attempt being a small fish in a big pond (deep tank)?

The latter would require them to develop new skills, but could facilitate their entry into the much bigger biopharma market. Biocon's ten-year association with Unilever had transformed the management mindset from a routine enzyme business to a quality-driven pharma business. Mazumdar-Shaw took a dramatic decision in 2006 to sell the company's foundational enzyme business to a top-class Danish company, Novozyme, which still operates the technology perfected by Biocon. Biocon embarked on the risky journey of biopharmaceuticals, a bit like a moulting bird preparing for flight.

She wanted to contribute to the battle against cancer by manufacturing breakthrough drugs based on monoclonal antibodies (MAB), but the technology was closely guarded by the Americans. An opportunity arose after she met a scientist from the Department of Molecular Biology of Cuba at a conference. Most people would have paid no heed to technology coming out of Cuba, since it had no existing reputation in the field of pharmaceutical innovation. Mazumdar-Shaw visited the Cuban laboratory, where the scientists expressed great interest in enhancing the value of their MAB technology. Biocon signed an agreement and, over the next decade, produced many novel drugs in collaboration with them. When Biocon embarked into the capital-intensive biopharma business, Mazumdar-Shaw chose the model of business partnerships and Biocon was able to taper the risks and enhance its rewards. The focus on 'value' over 'volume' was another conscious choice that Biocon made.

Such thinking was visible in other companies, too. In 1978, Tata Sons founded a JV with Burroughs, USA. F.C. Kohli, the then CEO, had two choices: either TCS could merge with the MNC or it could opt to develop as an independent start-up. Kohli decided to continue as a separate entity. In doing so, TCS had to learn to operate in a competitive environment, with freedom and creativity, and to work in foreign markets. The Burroughs arrangement had a clause which prevented TCS from seeking India-based clients. Kohli de-risked TCS by retaining key talent. His successor, S. Ramadorai, initiated a participative model of leadership and grew the company dramatically by embracing the challenge of Y2K.

At the HDFC group, Deepak Parekh always had his ear to the ground. Around 2005, HDFC decided to issue foreign currency convertible bonds (FCCBs) in Asia. It was a complex instrument. Pricing was crucial, since it was based on multiple variables like interest rate and foreign currency rates. The issue was global, and pricing was influenced by the judgement of US dollar and Japanese yen rates, the stock market sentiment and the conversion price five years hence. Using critical thinking, the price of INR 1,399 was determined. Whereas others' FCCBs had not been successful, HDFC's found tremendous success.

Kotak Mahindra Bank successfully weathered the 1997 Asian financial crisis. Out of the 4,000 non-bank financial services companies in India, only twenty survived, Kotak being one of them. Uday Kotak questioned every underlying assumption – a key trait of critical thinkers. While IDBI and IFCI were expanding their portfolios, Uday advised his team to do the opposite, just in case their assumptions went wrong. This saved the bank from catastrophe. Uday Kotak admits that he wanted to scale up and expand, but was equally cautious about risk, exemplifying a critical thinker. He shrank his capital lending base from INR 1,800 crore to INR 800 crore. Return *of* capital was more important than return *on* capital, he decided.

Project Lakshya was started by A.M. Naik at L&T with a perspective plan for ten years. The top 300 people in the company were tasked to decide where the company wanted to be in the future. Project Lakshya focused the energies of management on mega projects with a time frame of five years. The vision for five years under Project Lakshya was broken down further into yearly targets and quarterly targets, which was an important exercise.

Critical thinking demands excellent listening skills and encouraging arguments. Inferences are drawn with inductive and deductive thinking and a long-term perspective. It is about connecting the dots and constantly resetting the contours of one's thought processes.

Two more useful mantras for institution-building are 'orbit shifting' and 'cyclical learning'.

Orbit Shifting

An orbit is a predictable, repetitive pathway taken by celestial bodies, for example, the earth's orbit around the sun. Companies too settle into similarly predictable pathways. It requires special effort for them to change that pathway, in addition to a strong-willed leader who is willing to break free and change the orbit of a running organisation.

Anil Naik of L&T demonstrated grit and tenacity by deeply pondering the question: 'What should be done so that L&T enters the next orbit?' He focused his attention on the structural changes necessary to increase L&T's scale and redefine its scope. L&T had become the best in the country in its industry. Amid the globalisation buzz, the natural next step was to compete globally. ECC, the construction division of L&T, had gained some experience in constructing complex structures through its work in the Middle East and Gulf countries. L&T dreamt of entering the global market with heavy engineering equipment and hydrocarbon projects.

They needed to take a leap of faith and grow five to ten times larger to achieve the scale that a world-class heavy construction equipment manufacturer would require. Naik's team worked tirelessly to set up a new manufacturing facility near Hazira port so that they could export the large equipment by sea. Over the years, the orbit kept on shifting as Naik translated his macro vision into micro reality and transformed L&T.

The biggest block to orbit shifting of any form is mindset – which is, paradoxically, also its biggest enabler. Mindset change releases individuals and organisations to leapfrog beyond existing growth paradigms.

Marico was confronted with a challenge when a major competitor attacked its leading brand, Parachute, with Nihar in late 1990s. HUL backed Nihar with big ad spends, and the initial impact was substantial. Thereafter, Harsh Mariwala sat down with his team of consultants, but even after two intense days of creative brainstorming, nothing dramatic emerged.

On digging deeper, the management mindset was identified as an issue. The organisation had settled into a defensive mindset, and as a result, most of the thinking and ideas had been unconsciously guided by a defence mechanism. Once Marico's leadership confronted the real issue, they took a conscious decision to shift and think of an alternative approach. They worked with the powerful conviction that if they could not muster resources to compete effectively, they could win with their ideas. This mindset shift resulted in waves of innovation that led to Parachute acquiring the highest market share in its history. Marico even went on to acquire Nihar, a few years later.

Cyclical Learning

Cyclical learning is a simple learning mechanism that all of us follow almost intuitively. Cyclical learning means you act, make mistakes, review what went wrong and work on it again. But it is not simple for business leaders to follow. It takes a visionary to follow and practise this simple principle at the level of an organisation. Every business goes through cycles of boom and bust, but a shaper knows how to keep the business agile and navigate through the lows.

When HDFC had started as a housing mortgage company back in the 1970s, they had prised open a new market segment in India. There was no prior precedent to guide them on whether their customers would pay back or default. HDFC resorted to cyclical learning. They needed to choose their customers wisely to ensure borrowers had repayment capacity. They invested in training managers, sending them to the UK's building societies like Abbey National and Halifax, in order to learn about robust credit appraisal systems.

Once the company mastered housing finance through cyclical learning, they were ready to enter other financial services. HDFC entered banking, mutual funds, insurance, asset management, property funds, education loans – and the list is still growing. Clearly, HDFC has shifted orbit several times but learning by doing and cyclical learning remained at the core of its actions.

Much business research has been devoted to finding a mantra in the context of that company and that particular country. Several books have been written on how you can take your business from 'good to great' so it is 'built to last'. Naturally, readers are interested in learning a formula of what works, why and how.[5]

Organisational transformation must address all components – agenda, context and culture.

Breaking Barriers and Stakeholder Orientation

It is worth highlighting two more mindsets vital to successful transformation: (i) breaking barriers and (ii) stakeholder orientation.

Any transformation effort faces obstacles and barriers. The shaper seeks pearls of possibilities in the ocean of uncertainties, which are usually unseen and open up further opportunities. Seeing the big picture and trusting one's instincts requires high-impact, convergent actions in order to break barriers to transformation and growth. Once those rocks of resistance are broken, the barrage of changes serves as catalyst to create life-altering conditions, that is, new solutions emerge when the barriers are broken down. Here are some examples.

Hasmukhbhai Parekh registered HDFC as a housing mortgage company when he was sixty-six. It was the first Indian institution for housing finance. If executed well, it was a chance at social change. Dr Manmohan Singh, then Finance Secretary, doubted whether the idea would click. Hasmukhbhai remained enthusiastic about providing loans to the middle class to build their dream homes and even persuaded his nephew Deepak

Parekh to join his venture. Today, HDFC is the largest and most admired name among the financial institutions of India.

For twenty-three-year-old Uday Kotak, there was always the safety of the family business to return to. But he chose to throw himself into the bill discounting business and set up his first business with zero capital invested. One also needs to guard against legal or societal implications of breaking barriers. Bill discounting was eventually barred by regulators due to misuse by other operators. Some 60 per cent of Kotak's business vanished, so they ventured into the equipment leasing and capital markets. Kotak focused on increasing value and not volume. Growth must add economic value. It was action from a renewed mindset that helped Kotak transform from being a small bank to among India's most valuable banks.

At Biocon, Mazumdar-Shaw had to break through many social barriers, especially gender. Job applicants were hesitant to join her as they perceived a lack of job security in working for a woman. Lending institutions did not have faith in a woman entrepreneur investing in technology which was unheard of in those days. Due to her strong sense of purpose, she overcame many barriers to make Biocon an admired biotech company globally. While most Indian pharma companies focused on generics, Mazumdar-Shaw focused on more risky businesses. She was the first to start research services on biosimilars through Syngene.

Breaking barriers requires purpose, confidence, risk-taking abilities and risk mitigation to escape the gravitational forces of habitual thinking.

Stakeholder Orientation

The values and interests of the various stakeholders of organisations, for example, employees, customers, shareholders, communities, suppliers, etc., are often in conflict with each other and need to be balanced, harmonised, integrated and aligned. Stakeholders are living, breathing human beings eager for human connection.

Stakeholder orientation is cultural and behavioural insofar as organisational members need to be continuously aware of and proactively act on a variety of stakeholder issues. Institution builders concurrently create value for all. As per the stakeholder theory, propounded by Edward Freeman in 1984, creating value requires challenge, critique and imagination to handle potential conflicts.[6] Such an orientation requires a deep and abiding focus on the purpose, not just profits. This helps institutions operate in a pragmatic, sustainable, responsible and ethical way. Examples follow.

TCS stands out for its prominence in all respects. The Tata Business Excellence Model or TBEM, as mentioned before, was driven to deliver strategic direction and drive business improvements which have connected the company with its suppliers, customers and partners. The company slogan, 'Experience certainty', involved all stakeholders through a commitment to deliver credible results.

Biocon's purpose of accessible innovation for affordable healthcare focuses on billions of patients rather than billions of dollars. Biocon partnered with Mylan and other international pharma players to improve the reach of the company's drugs in the global markets. Biocon's efforts for improving community health sharply aligned with stakeholders' interests. Employees develop positive learning abilities, knowing that their employer is satisfying all stakeholders. Global hiring was also undertaken to build requisite capabilities.

At Marico, contributing to the good of society is important. Neither the company nor its stakeholders pollute the environment. Marico's coconut collection centres provide cultivation-related information to the farmers. Outreach programmes focusing on scientific farming practices help raise farmer incomes.

The descriptions of these two mindsets and actions, along with corporate examples, illustrate how organisations create a new narrative for institution building. In this book, we illustrate two dimensions of institution building: short versus long term and levers of change.

Short Term versus Long Term

Managing the short and long terms simultaneously is a great challenge for many leaders. Both are necessary and important for institution building, but how does a leader do both?

Marico's value statement affirms 'profit optimisation'. This signals that there will be no trade-off between quality and costs for short-term benefits. For Harsh Mariwala, this commitment meant that the gap between revenues and profits was acceptable so long as the growth line was steeper than the loss line. Marico avoided the common practice of month-end loading of stocks into its channel. Mariwala ensured this by installing an integrated management information system (MIS) that linked supply to channel sales. This commitment to the trade has had a beneficial impact on Marico's long-term profitability.

At Kotak Mahindra Bank, Uday Kotak's policy was to take baby steps: 'It will be slower, but success will be more solid and sustainable.' All decisions were based on an underlying criterion of value creation. Kotak would often say, 'If something did not create economic value, Kotak Mahindra Bank would not do it just to boost the next quarter earnings.'[7]

Anil Naik, too, was cast from the same mould at L&T. Even as the manufacturing facility at Hazira was taking shape, Naik kept looking ahead and got working simultaneously on getting skilled workers, by putting in place a masterplan for sourcing and training labour: the hardscape. This refers to creating capacity by way of a massive fabrication yard and installing machinery; he also focused on the softscape, or capability building and training manpower, simultaneously.

Naik's grasp of the fundamental truth of short-term actions building up to generate long-term value is revealed in his unremitting commitment towards ensuring that long-term share price reflected the true value of L&T. The true value of a share is determined by growth of business, along with profitability and return of capital employed. Naik launched Project Blue Chip, a programme to successfully transform L&T into a blue chip company.

Levers of Change

A shaper anticipates and exploits emerging trends across all functional areas to galvanise the organisation's movement from complacency to an aspirational mindset.

Perceiving the emerging consumer trend of inclination towards 'brands' in the 1980s, Mariwala engineered Marico's shift from the traditional business mindset of selling a product to the market to the professional mindset of marketing a brand to the customer. He transformed Parachute cooking oil from a commodity to a differentiated brand through innovative packaging, customised offerings and direct retailing. At the organisational level, Harsh leveraged the soft power of the human resource function to reshape Marico as an empowered and responsible family of hierarchy-unconscious members, energised by the organisational belief 'you win or you learn'.

At L&T, Anil Naik perceived human resources as a lever of change for institutionalising employee commitment. Naik was conscious of the strong sense of emotional bonding encoded in the managers of L&T, reflecting the professional values of the founders and many leaders. Under his leadership, a win-win scheme was devised to convert the emotional equity of the employees to financial equity. This was done by hiving off the cement unit to the Aditya Birla Group and transferring the transaction amount to L&T Employees' Welfare Trust. As the company did not have a single owner with a large shareholding, this action served to ring-fence L&T from corporate raiders, with employees now having substantial voting rights.

At Kotak Mahindra Bank, Uday Kotak adopted digital technology as a prime lever of change for rapid onboarding of customers with zero account balance, through the simple process of a banking app. Kotak Mahindra Bank's investment in IT from the start-up stage enabled it to leverage the first-mover advantage when the Reserve Bank of India brought in the video-based Know Your Customer option, and when insurance and mutual fund operations were opened up for banks.

Enterprise, Education and Eudaemonia

Entrepreneurship, education and eudaemonia (Greek term for 'well-being') are all highly relevant to the progress of human society, specifically India. Why so?

From the earliest days of Aristotle and Kautilya, philosophers have lauded the crucial role of business in building a happy, prosperous society. Indians have inherited a rich business tradition which has been excellently documented: Chettiars of Tamil Nadu, Moplahs of Kerala in the south; Marwaris of Rajasthan, Kutchis of Saurashtra and Sindhis – who live everywhere. Business traditions are a part of local folklore all over the country.

Business generates profit; after honest payment of taxes, this results in merchant charity through community support – temples, wells, hospitals, schools, fine arts and support to advance local entrepreneurship. In this way, enterprise enables education, culture and health. Together, these three are the ingredients of human well-being and a happy society – what the Greeks called 'eudaemonia'. Stated another way, a good society needs vigorous enterprise which can generate resources to promote administrative order. In this manner, citizens can enjoy education, health, cultural advancement and a sense of well-being.

Thus, honest business is good for society. While history describes the role of business in these terms, we also need to consider the contemporary role of business in the future of India. Some citizens are rightly disappointed by the excesses and greed of some businesspeople. However, such mistrust should not be applied to all businesspeople alike. A diatribe against business is as misplaced as a congenital mistrust in politicians, bureaucrats, activists, journalists and lawyers as entire classes. Small businesses must flourish; some will grow into larger and competitive companies, which, in turn, must grow into 'business institutions'. Such a progression is good for society.

The stock market, set up in 1875, has 5,000 listed companies, but only 2,000 are traded and a small set of 'business institutions' account for over half the market capitalisation. India desperately needs more business institutions for its economic progress – we would be much better placed if there were many more valuable, virile, value-based companies. Needless to say, this will go on to be an integral part of the solution for the progress of the Indian economy.

Summary

- Like human beings, companies are also subject to mortality.
- The principles of a healthy, adaptive life for human beings are also relevant for a healthy, adaptive company.
- Healthy, adaptive companies have great practices in (i) unleashing people power; (ii) maintaining short-term focus along with long-term; and (iii) practising critical thinking.
- The Brahma mantra or the essence of the message is that it does take a lot for companies to stay healthy and adaptive for as long as they live, as detailed in this chapter. Such is the soft science of transformation.

Part 2

The Strategic Aspects of Transformation

Hrishi Bhattacharyya

7
Hindsight for Foresight

The best and the most revered presidents and prime ministers of countries become legendary for their knowledge of history, appreciation of culture, grasp of the present, ambition for the future and how one might attain it. They are usually obsessive leaders who want to embrace the future. These qualities, coincidentally, also characterise the best CEOs of companies everywhere, though it is a rare breed.

In our lifetimes, we have seen many CEOs, in India and elsewhere, who spent all their time micro-managing the quarterly bottom line, focusing on cost-cutting, promotional activities, flexing supply chains, fiats and orders. Oftentimes they created an atmosphere of fear and insecurity. In extreme cases, short-term results were declared through a combination of fudging and corruption. Such people did not last long but did unredeemable damage to their organisations in their limited tenures.

When we began our careers in HLL in the late 1960s, it was essentially a supply game – the more you produced, the more you could sell. The constraint was not consumer choice but the 'licence raj', other regulatory impediments and a unionised workforce. The strategy was simple: to raise machine and labour productivity, increase production capacities, ensure raw materials procurement, work with the union leaders, and manage Delhi. Factory managers had the right skills to implement the business needs, and four of them – Vasant

Rajadhakshya, T. Thomas, Ashok Ganguly and Susim Datta – one after another, went on to become CEOs of the company.

If the story ended there, HLL would be just an ordinary company. The reason it became extraordinary is that it implemented several 'counter-intuitive' strategies simultaneously: despite shortages, Bhau Phansalkar (later General Sales Manager) started appointing dedicated distributors instead of relying fully on market wholesalers to evenly and widely distribute products and even ration brands like Sunlight and Lifebuoy to create great respect in the grocery trade as a fair, honest, reliable supplier who brought these valued products to the shopkeepers' door every week without fail. Ranjan Banerjee (later Head of Personnel), along with his deputies Tarun Sheth and R.R. Nair, recruited and trained the best available talent from IITs and Indian Institutes of Management (IIMs), when no such qualification was immediately required. Dr Varadarajan, the first R&D Director, set up a research centre as early as 1966. Max Vatsal (later Marketing Manager), having mapped public water supply nationally, realised that India had hard water and soap formulations were not the best for washing clothes – this later led to the genesis of the detergent bar Rin (in 1969) which was many times more efficient. Dr Vasant Patankar led consumer research, operations research and IT teams. Rajesh Bahadur (Controller, Personal Products [PP]), Hrishikesh Bhattacharyya (Senior Product Manager), Nihal Kaviratne (General Sales Manager, PP) and Gerson da Cunha (CEO and Creative Head, Lintas) leapfrogged from matrimonial advertisements to the creation of Fair & Lovely (in 1975) to build a totally new market segment in personal products.

The point of these stories is that HLL of the 1970s, while efficiently and skilfully managing its present, was also consciously preparing for change. It wanted to remain fit and ready for the future. Strategy must draw from the past, deal with the present and prepare for the future.

Why Only Some Succeed

Many well-known global companies were smart, too. Jeff Bezos started Amazon in 1994 armed with foresight. He sensed that combining the newly emerging internet, increased desktop sales, higher penetration of credit cards, technology innovations in logistics and an offer to deliver directly to people's homes could create a new superior business model in book retailing. Finding the business model to be robust, he expanded both the product portfolio and geography of operations at high speed. Others were not so smart. Sears, which started in 1893, had virtually invented the mail order business. All they had to do to get a head start was digitise their catalogue and start commerce over the internet. But they spectacularly failed to see emerging trends. In fact, in a cruel twist of fate, they shut down the mail order division in 1993 – a year before Jeff Bezos founded Amazon! Walmart, which started in 1962, had built a great infrastructure in the next thirty years, with a network of depots and stores which opened all over small towns and rural America. David Glass, who succeeded founder Sam Walton in 1988, was busy expanding into supercentres and internationally and presiding over the first US$1 billion in sales; he had all the scale and global resources at his command. Despite having all these advantages, Walmart failed to spot the emerging potential. They probably judged that Bezos as a bookseller was just a competitor to Barnes and Noble. Wealth in current times does not protect the future of a business; foresight does. Today, although Walmart has built a US$80 billion business online, it trails Amazon by six times – their respective market shares in online retailing are 6.3 per cent and 37.8 per cent.[1]

Accurate forecasts have always been taken seriously by managers. When we joined HLL as fresh graduates from IIT (Gopal) and IIM (Hrishi), the state of that art was very rudimentary, indeed. Population, GDP, inflation, trade offtake-based market data and so on were available, but with considerable time lag. No one was analysing them anyway. Internal sales data is all we had. Data availability was not only limited but everything had to be computed manually. We brought some science into play by introducing concepts like moving annual totals and presenting them visually. Fortunately, everything was very slow-moving (except the growth in population) and the forecasts made turned out to be reasonably accurate. At that time, the past was a good predictor of the future.

Fast forward to the new millennium – the progress of science and technology, digitisation and computing power have triggered a fresh industrial revolution. Change was upon us in a big and unprecedented way, and before we knew it, linear programming of data became a rather blunt tool. As Thomas Friedman explained in his book *The World Is Flat*,[2] countries and businesses had to grapple with a new set of fast-changing circumstances.

In the next chapter we explain that the future is not going to be a straightforward extrapolation of the past. One must still deeply understand the past and carry its lessons into the future, while also being prepared to shed a lot of baggage.

Summary

- Understanding the past is deeply important. Assimilating it well and drawing core lessons from it is even more important. That is hindsight. This not only covers data and events, but also the culture and value systems of the organisation.
- Extrapolation of the past into the future in a linear way was a game one could play safely in the twentieth century, when growth was lower, competition was milder and technological innovation was slower – but not any more.
- Change, even runaway change, characterises the world of business today. One needs to learn to cope with it; even benefit from it.

- To do the above, one needs to learn from the past, manage the present and prepare for the future. We must imagine the future we want, and then fold it in into the present.

8

Future

How Much Like the Past Will It Be?

This is a story explaining why traditional tools of industry analysis and competition analysis fail to deliver transformational strategies. There is a simple reason for it: the future is not going to be like the past.

It was a nice June day in London. The sun was streaming in through the large windows of the faculty lunchroom at the London Business School (LBS), and I was waiting to welcome Dilip Doshi (name changed), who was visiting the city. Doshi, an old business acquaintance from my Mumbai days, was a successful CEO who had inherited an office automation business from his father. After the usual pleasantries, I found that Mr Doshi was looking somewhat glum and distracted. 'Is anything the matter?' I asked. He blurted out, 'Professor Bhattacharyya, please block a few days for us during your next visit to India. We need you to develop a new strategy', he said.

Not fully surprised, as I have had similar conversations with other CEOs, I asked, 'Why do you need a new strategy?' He looked grim again. 'Our market share is falling, even our sales are declining, and at the same time, a major competitor is aggressively innovating.' He continued, 'It is a perfect storm. Our profits are down and margins are under pressure. The business is very much in a crisis.' To calm him down, I ordered another glass of Chablis for him. After a longish pause, he pleaded, 'Professor, can you help us transform the business so that we can again face the future with confidence?'

Some more minutes passed in silence. 'What is your current strategy, and can I see a document?' I finally asked. Mr Doshi replied, 'Yes, we do have one, and here is a bound set of documents from a previous consultant that I have brought for you.'

'Did you follow it?' I persisted.

'Not in its entirety,' Doshi said, 'but it is useless anyway, as it is not working, and our business results are all in trouble.' I promised to meet with him and his team in Mumbai.

Relieved, Doshi promised, 'I will arrange to send you all our data prior to your visit.' A couple of weeks later, UPS delivered a bulky envelope which contained weekly sales, monthly market shares, P&L and margin statements, and lots of major competitors' data. Customer data? Yes, there were some product test results as well.

All strategy exercises are an attempt to keep the business relevant well into the future, to address the next set of needs and wants of its various stakeholders, over a period which could be short, like two years, or somewhat longer, like five years or more.

The question left on the table then is: If we are working to create a future, why is all our data and understanding about the past? Our knowledge and understanding can bring us, at best, only to the present, but mostly keep us locked in the past. If we exclusively use quantitative methods and extrapolate, are we going to get the right answers for tomorrow and the day after? If we think of competitors only from the present time, the ones with whom we grapple today, are we making the right assumptions in a fast-changing world?

Having said this, there is no excuse for not fully understanding the past and the present, and how they might be useful and relevant in the future. One *must* go through the exercise for objectively understanding the starting point.

Strategy Development Techniques

Four familiar processes, which remain contemporary, are: SWOT analysis, industry and competition analyses, benchmarking competition, and war games.

SWOT simply stands for: Strengths, Weaknesses, Opportunities and Threats. It is a good starting exercise. However, when working the matrix, one tends to do a better job with an articulation of their strengths and weaknesses, and a weaker job with opportunities and threats. And, unfortunately, it is all imagined within a current industry definition – which often becomes an intrinsic and fatal error.

Industry analysis

The thinking on how to analyse one's 'playing field' was developed by Michael Porter over forty years ago, in 1979, and remains to this day a valid and much-needed exercise. Both authors were fortunate to have learnt this directly from Professor Porter himself, when we attended the Advanced Management Program at Harvard Business School in the 1990s. What it says, at its core, is that one's industry is subjected to five forces – all external to the company – and the organisation needs to recognise those forces before developing what can be a winning strategy.

What are these five forces? The first of them is 'competitive rivalry'. Some industries have many players, high production capacities and undifferentiated products. Though easy to enter because of low entry barriers, there is always intense pricing and margin pressure – generally not an attractive place to be in. On the other hand, if there are few players, a potentially large market because of high growth, differentiated products and stable supply of materials, expansion with good profitability, is the likelier outcome.

The next are the bargaining powers of suppliers and customers. Many suppliers obviously have less bargaining power and material costs tend to be lower. Supply lines are also generally assured and the chance of breakdown in production is considerably low. If one company has a problem maintaining supplies, another would be easily available, and most often at the same or lower prices. The opposite is true when suppliers are few and their products are technically complex, or even proprietary. Such suppliers have much strength and high bargaining power with their customers.

Customers have power if they have high market share and, therefore, large volumes. Also, when there is overcapacity, and many suppliers are trying to get to the large customers. When the materials are generally undifferentiated, there are plenty of substitutes available and that is a situation that customers can exploit by pitting one supplier against another.

The next force proposed by Porter is the 'threat of new entrants'. Is someone planning a large capital expenditure coupled with product innovation? That could be a significant threat to the current players in the market. If the end customers are dissatisfied and are looking for something new, manufacturers have an interest to invest in the next round of possible innovation, and suppliers have an opportunity for differentiation.

The last of them is the 'threat of substitute products', which is quite self-explanatory.

Porter offered two generic strategies. One was cost leadership. By finding a way to have least cost compared to competition, companies could have greater pricing freedom, without affecting margins. Cost leadership also often leads to the second generic strategy, namely, differentiation. Low cost compared to other players kept margins intact and generated resources to invest into product innovation, leading to differentiation and thus greater demand for their products.

Benchmarking

Another popular analysis to generate a winning strategy is through a process called 'benchmarking competition'. This is, put simply, a process of taking key business metrics and comparing them. This can be done internally to see differences in productivity of different parts of a business, and thereafter trying to streamline superior practices across the board. This exercise is often done by comparing oneself to a major competitor.

The term 'benchmarking' for business was coined by Robert Camp at Xerox (1979). When the company realised (to their horror) that competitors – mainly the Japanese, like Canon – were selling copy machines well below Xerox's production costs, they started a benchmarking study for its production department with the objective of getting more competitive. Such an exercise is very difficult to do accurately, as correct data is not easily or publicly available, and thus the exercise starts depending on too many subjective elements. If done well, such efforts at benchmarking can lead to a good understanding of best industry practices. Unfortunately, even when done well, it brings one only to the present.

War games

Among the popular strategy-generating exercises, the last that I would like to cover is called 'war games'. I first played it in a strategy planning retreat in Jakarta for the Personal Products division of Unilever Indonesia. This has been, as the name suggests, borrowed from war-planning exercises. It is typically held in a group situation, where each group consisting of four to six people is asked to think of themselves as a company unit which will either go to war with a particular competitor or will defend itself from an attack by that competitor. By watching how the competitor attacks you successfully, you gauge the infirmities of your own strategy. If you are attacking a competitor and he defends himself well, you assess their true strengths.

This exercise is energising and creates a lot of passion as the cry of war and subsequent win is a feel-good activity. However, it is played in the present with current knowledge;

therefore, the outcomes tend to be more tactical rather than strategic. The ideas put on the table are often outlandish, risky and impractical. Unfortunately, this is often a distracting use of time, which could be more productively spent in thinking of how to serve one's customers better. I have rarely seen a sensible CEO accepting the suggestions that are presented at the end of a 'war game' day. Once again, finding accurate competitive data is a serious challenge.

Of these, Porter's model is the most scholarly, practical and doable. However, its main analytical usefulness lies in times of decision-making, especially when considering whether to enter or exit an industry. When one tries and uses the process to create a new strategy, one often feels underequipped to articulate a strong one. Generic strategies come easily, but one needs to be more specific and sharper to take on key competitors.

I am not against doing any of these exercises – I have indeed done them on many occasions as a starting point to get an objective, data-based understanding of what the past has been and what the present is, in an industry. It has the ability, if done well, to bring one to the present. It is thus a necessary but not a sufficient exercise. Our job is to create a strategy for tomorrow and the day after; not for yesterday and the day before. And the future is most often different from the past, unless one is living in a stable, low-growth, low-innovation period. Mathematics, statistics, and other quantitative methods allow one to make projections as well; but they are of value only when the future is likely to be more like the past.

Limited Value in Today's World

There are two major strategic reasons why these exercises have limited usefulness in today's business environment to articulate what we should do in the future for a relevant and winning solution. The first is industry definition, and the second is change and the rate of change.

Let us examine them one by one. Why is it that it is becoming increasingly difficult to state what industry one is in? The reason is that a lot of the innovation today is about 'bundling', which successfully blurs old industry definitions.

Take the case of phones. Not that many years ago, we could make calls and receive calls within a locale. The phone sat on a desk in the office or on a table at home. You could, with the help of an operator, talk long distance, even overseas, with your business contacts, family, relatives and friends. And if one was going to be away from the phone, the caller could record incoming messages with the help of another gadget – a recorder. This was great progress of technology and was rightfully called an industry.

What are the smartphones of today? First, it is no more a bulky device encumbered with wires and plug points, installed in your home or office. It is a small, sleek mobile gadget that one carries in one's pocket or purse, and if someone has your number, they can reach you wherever you are. So the question is: Does a smartphone still do its primary job and allow one to make and receive calls? Yes, of course it does. But it also shows time (watch), date (calendar), appointments (diary), sends and receives emails and texts (telex and fax), connects to the internet (computer), takes pictures and videos (camera), stores and plays music (record player), stores and plays movies (cinema projector), stores files (filing cabinet), plays presentations (slide projector), makes deposits and payments (banking app) and orders products (online retail app). This is an illustrative not a comprehensive list. And I have not even mentioned the numerous other apps that help one access multiple services.

What one can easily see is that this one little product in our hand or pocket, which most of us almost take for granted now (as there are over 7 billion of them[1] and then the billions of internet connections that reside within them), has collapsed at least a dozen distinct products and industries. And who are their competitors now? There are hundreds of them. But is one competing against other watches? Or other cameras? Or other document storage systems? Or banking services?

Some may argue that the smartphone is a unique product and service and does not represent a new operating pattern to redefine what we have known and understood in the past. So let us give another example of a visible and successful application.

Let us go into an American kitchen. And what do we see there? A Ninja air fryer, for example.

What can such a product do? It is a pressure cooker, a slow cooker, an air fryer, a steamer, a sauté pan, a roaster, a mini oven, a broiler and a dehydrator. It is an appliance designed to consolidate the cooking and preparing of food within one device. How many industries and products has it collapsed into one? More than ten, if you read their advertisement. And how many competitors resided in those traditional industries? Over a hundred, for sure. Many of those may not go forward any more. So how do you apply the traditional techniques and logic of strategy development?

The second big factor to be considered is change and the rate of change.

Anecdotally, one feels that a lot of change is happening on the demographic, technology, political and social fronts. However, as one day merges into the next, one rarely feels the movement and how it is changing our lives. To understand and measure the impact and consequences on the business world, we need to look back and see what happened.

We are at the start of a new century. The start of the millennium was just about twenty years ago, when many of us remember feeling nervous about Y2K and whether all computers would stop operating on one fateful day. Well, that did not happen. But the changes that did happen over this short period of twenty years are massive and almost unfathomable by past standards.

Massive Doses of Change

Demographics

Since the year 2000, 1.2 billion people have died – a big number – but 3 billion babies were born. The global population had thus grown from 6.1 billion to 8 billion by November 2022.[2] This simple statistic means that we have 3 billion more mouths to feed, to provide with adequate nutrition, educate, and impart skills to, which they will need as they start entering the workforce. A mighty resource is in our hands, but so also are the seeds of how they will – or will not – integrate into their respective societies.

The staggering number of 1 billion deaths, mostly caused by cardiac and respiratory diseases and cancer, points to how much we still need to achieve in the area of medical sciences and hospital care, despite the impressive strides we have already made. India and China both have a population of 1.4 billion each, that is, one out of every three people in the world is either Indian or Chinese, or 35 per cent of the total worldwide number. With rising incomes and aspirations, what will be the most logical playing fields for business? How does a Western mindset successfully cater to the needs and wants of these uniquely Asian consumers?

Though 3 billion people are twenty years or less in age, the world is ageing. It is estimated that we now have 1 billion people who are sixty or over. How different are their needs? This grey population, either retired or nearing retirement, with reasonable wealth at their disposal but with emerging chronic ailments and increasingly limited mobility – but still young, mentally, and wanting to enjoy life to the fullest – will produce numerous business opportunities in housing, entertainment, travel and healthcare, just to name a few, to cater to this large, ever-expanding market.

Urbanisation

The other demographic trend worth noting is that the population is moving towards cities. In 2000, 50 per cent of the global population (3 billion) lived in cities; today, the number is 55 per cent (4.4 billion). It is estimated that two out of three people will live in cities by 2050 (66 per cent of 9.8 billion = 6.5 billion).[3]

Energy

Energy needs will keep increasing. In the past twenty years, energy supply has grown from 9,900 thermal energy units (TES) to 14,000 TES.[4] And there are still numerous energy-deficient and dark places around the globe waiting to gain access to modern amenities. How do we supply this large need, and more importantly, in a less polluting and more sustainable way? The answer is emerging.

Traditional sources of energy are fossil fuels like coal. Crude oil and natural gas, which triggered the First Industrial Revolution, continue to be extremely important. China meets 50 per cent of its requirements by mining coal. The second source is nuclear energy that comes from uranium. But the third, and most important source for the future, will come from renewable sources.

Renewables include biomass, hydropower, solar, tidal and wind sources. These clean energy supplies contributed less than 1 per cent of energy supplies in the year 2000, when consumption was 9,900 TES. That number has risen by 13 per cent in 2022, with a base of 14,000 TES. China, despite its enormous dependence on coal, generates 10 per cent of its needs from renewables; in India, 33 per cent of energy usage comes from renewables.[5] This rise and fall in generation costs every year will revolutionise energy supply and consumption during the Fourth Industrial Revolution that is in its infancy now.

Connectivity

Though connectivity felt immense at the turn of the century, especially if one lived in the developed Western world, by today's standards, it was tiny. There were only 361 million internet connections in 2000. But how easy was it to get a connection and what was the typical speed when you got one? Just twenty years ago, connecting to the internet meant enduring the beautiful screeching of a 56k dial-up modem as it established a connection; it was also painstakingly slow with a terrible user interface and horrid design.

I remember when I started teaching MBA students in 2003, at the University of Michigan Business School, Ann Arbor, that is just what I had to do. And what was the internet speed at that time? Traditional dial-up modems have largely disappeared, but the download speeds then were around 10 Mbps, and uploads were just impractical. Emails were drafted and stacked up in the outbox and sent all together when one got an internet connection. The telephone line and the internet could not be used at the same time. Nevertheless, we were still very excited that we could use those technologies at all.

In 2022, there were over 5 billion internet connections. This is almost 65 per cent of the global population. China alone has 1.02 billion users; the US by comparison has just 307 million. India, the second largest, has 750 million. Compare this to twenty years ago, when internet users were mainly institutions, places of higher learning, research centres and large businesses. When it comes to speed, the global average download speed on fixed broadband is 113.25 Mbps on fixed broadband and 63.15 Mbps on mobile today. This change has had a tremendous impact on our lives and on our businesses and democratised commerce.

Wireless devices

Innovations in rechargeable battery technology fuelled the proliferation of many devices which did not need a wire, a plug or an electrical wall socket any more to function. Batteries are the reason why mobility has been ushered in for so many everyday devices. Of course, batteries need to be periodically charged.

The other invention is Wi-Fi. Few of us can imagine a life when the internet was not available on our phones, watches, or computers. But it was invented only in 1997 and is barely twenty-five years old. Many of us older people have lived most of our lives without that instant access.

Google

Not long ago, students spent hours in libraries, scientists read papers and books to assist their research and we carried paper maps while travelling by road and needed a knowledgeable person to answer our questions. Today, this is all available not only at your desk but wherever you are, on your phone or tablet. It has made a profound impact on our lives, but this too came into being only in 1998. Since then, Wi-Fi and internet speeds have brought this repository of information into the hands of many billion.

Online shopping

The availability of high-speed internet and parallel expansion of modes of payment over the internet has led to a revolution in retailing. In 2000, online sales were estimated to be US$44.5 billion.[6] In just twenty years, the value has risen to US$5.5 trillion, that is, by more than ten times. Did Jeff Bezos know when he started Amazon in 1994 that this would happen? He surely must have had a feeling in his gut. His sales in 2000, six years after he first began, were US$2.7 billion – not bad for a start-up. In 2021, Amazon sales were US$ 470 billion and its profits were US$ 33 billion.

Social media

Also, riding on the back of the internet is social media. At the start of the millennium, the only thing close to modern-day social media was the AOL instant messenger. Email, though invented in 1976, remained dormant for many years, and yet by the 1990s, it had become common in business, governance, universities and defence/military. Starting with the advent of webmail (the web-era form of email) and email clients in the mid-1990s, use of email began to extend to the rest of the public. By 2000, we were sending and receiving 1.5 billion messages a day. Today, after twenty years, at least 320 billion emails are sent and received every day.[7]

Facebook started in 2004 (as FaceMash in 2003) and allowed everyone over thirteen years of age to use it in 2006. Mark Zuckerberg founded Facebook on 4 February 2004, together with a few Harvard classmates, and was the first one to create an official Facebook profile with ID no. 4. From that one user sixteen years ago, more than two-thirds of all Americans are now on Facebook (243 million).[8] But the largest base of its users is in India, with 330 million users. The global number of monthly users is more than 3 billion. Yet another profound influence on people, society, culture, politics, and business. If one takes all social media users, Kepios estimates that there are 4.7 billion social media users around the world, equivalent to 59 per cent of the population. Social media users have also continued to grow in 2023, with over 200 million new users entering this craze.

Gig economy

Twenty years ago, almost all working people were employed full-time and attached to a single company. We had contracts binding us to a single organisation. 'Moonlighting' was a dirty word, and violators were either dismissed or could be legally punished. It was a large part of retaining information and secrecy. In 2020, we have a new labour market with short-term contracts or freelance work, as opposed to permanent jobs. The global value of this market is estimated at over US$2 trillion, and estimates show that almost a third (36 per cent) of all American workers are participants.[9] A large proportion of these people say that it is their primary job. Even I became a part of this fledgling market in 2003, when I accepted my first consulting contract after my retirement from Unilever, where I had worked on a permanent, full-time basis for thirty-five years.

There was a stigma attached, at one time, to part-time work, and even those who were working that way wanted to put a quick end to it with a permanent position. People doing part-time work were generally very insecure, as their income flows were uneven, and being able to provide for the family and pay rent or mortgages was a constant concern.

Again, the current trends herein will have profound impact on how business is done. Being able to get a skill base that one needs, without having to hire permanently, means being able to stay on top of knowledge in any given area. On the other hand, how do you motivate and energise people who are with you on a purely transactional basis?

TV, cable and streaming

Streaming has made video available on demand. And along with Wi-Fi, you can access it on mobile devices anytime, anywhere. Streaming, invented around 1992, languished for many years as the internet bandwidth available made it an unstable product, with frequent loss of picture and buffering. That changed with the advent of Netflix, which was launched in 2006. In ten years, they had gone worldwide, spreading to 130 countries.[10] Today, in America, a third of all TV viewership is through streaming, with cable being a close second, followed by broadcast at 21 per cent. TV viewership in 2020 is estimated to be over 5 billion globally, and has no doubt expanded through the combination of broadcast, cable and streaming. In 2000, the number of TV viewers was 3.8 billion, with the major chunk coming from broadcast television.

The changes listed above are merely illustrative, and not exhaustive by any means. Some of the ones selected here are just to better assert the point that change is everywhere, in all the different aspects of our life, and affecting the world of business in multiple ways. The changes are also happening very fast. Twenty years is a very short time in the history of modern civilisation, but the rate of change is so fast that people are now getting exposed to things that they could not even have imagined when young.

Change and Interdependence

The other aspect of change are the interdependencies among them. Take online shopping, for example. This form of doing business needs access to computers or mobile devices, the availability of the internet, Wi-Fi services, the development of web design and services, high-speed broadband, improved productivity of home delivery services, and access to credit cards. Without all of them, the business model does not form a closed loop. Jeff Bezos was right in starting Amazon only in 1994. Many of the things mentioned above were just starting to happen or were in their infancy. It could not have been given shape in 1984 – just ten years earlier.

Will change continue to happen? And will the pace of change continue to be the same, too? These are important questions which business strategies for the future will have to address.

We believe that each passing decade will be full of important changes that will impact many aspects of human life, and business management will not stand as an exception to that rule.

Three Different but Mutually Interactive Changes

I believe that all changes which are relevant to the world of business can be conceptually grouped into three buckets. These changes are different, but mutually interactive, leading to value creation. It can be conceived as a cycle of change vectors that will influence and trigger change in the other two vectors when one is changed. These are: (i) consumer needs priority change; (ii) new technology inventions; and (iii) business design innovations. Let us try and understand them one by one, and then all together.

Consumer needs priority change

The base of consumer needs remains practically the same, like the need to brush one's teeth every morning and at bedtime. The products needed to accomplish this simple task are toothpaste and a toothbrush. But for a while, we want teeth whitening more than other things, or elimination of bad breath, or gum care, or taking care of sensitivity. There may be different segments of toothpaste users that always prefer teeth whitening over gum care, and so on. This is what marketers understand from studying consumers and provide different formulations and brands to meet those needs. This continued for a very long time until one day, Colgate realised that consumers were, at their core, unhappy to trade off one of these needs over another, as they valued them equally and needed them all. Thus emerged the concept of Colgate Total, which challenged the existing segmentation of the market. This understanding of the change in priority of the toothpaste user resulted in the runaway success of the newly launched product. Similar logic has developed the battery-operated toothbrushes that give the consumer a newer experience in oral hygiene.

New technology inventions

The stream of new technologies come predominantly due to the furtherance of knowledge by scientists and researchers. Every single day, in laboratories around the world, increasing numbers of smart people are seeking solutions to improve productivity or to reduce cost. Any one of these, often created or targeted towards a specific industry or business at the start, spreads its wings and influences many industries and businesses. Think of applications in robotics, energy generation, human genome mapping, batteries, telephony, photography and imaging, internet speeds and so on.

Let us look at the progress of just one new technology: mobile standards. Technically, this began in 1973, when the first mobile call was made. But the real start was around 1990, when 1G (first generation) became available, first in Japan, and soon thereafter in the US, Canada and the UK. It had poor reach and a lot of background noise. Nevertheless, it garnered 20 million global subscribers. In the ten years between 1991 and 2001, first the 2G and then the four times faster 3G standards were launched. This allowed text messages to be sent, and later multimedia messages. With 3G data packets driving web connectivity being standardised, seamless global transfers of voice, data and pictures were allowed. You could now have videoconferencing and video streaming. 4G and 5G got launched in the ten years between 2010 and 2020. In which areas of industry and business will this technology have the most impact? The most obvious one is manufacturing, but it will also greatly impact agriculture, healthcare, transport and education, to name just a few.

Business design innovations

These are innovations that companies make in their operations, which improve productivity or reduce costs, or both. Typically, areas of change are new product development, manufacturing and processes, logistics, financing systems, distribution methodologies and others.

My personal favourite is from the book-retailing industry and what Amazon did at inception in the mid-1990s. Brick-and-mortar booksellers had two major costs – store rent and book inventory. When the store owner bought books from the publisher or wholesaler, he got thirty days' credit. But the titles he bought sold on an average in ninety days, and so he had to cover inventory for sixty days. By creating a virtual store, from where you bought online, Amazon eliminated the costly rentals on high streets. And by collecting for the title sold by credit card, he got the sales proceeds immediately, but continued to receive credit from his suppliers. His ongoing business was fully financed by his customers at zero per cent interest rates, and he only had to invest new money to finance growth. This business system advantage acquired over all existing booksellers truly restructured the market.

The beauty of this is that all three are equal centres of change. Change can be triggered by customers, technology or business systems. And if changes happen in one of them in any significant way, that unleashes a force of change in the other two. I will explain this in more detail later in the book.

All this content, with greater elaboration and interactivity, was presented and discussed over two days, with a senior multifunctional group, in the Mumbai offices of Dilip Doshi, during my visit to India. Slowly but surely, all in attendance understood the need for understanding the past as well as the lag inherent in known techniques to forecast accurately. They also had a new mindset – the confidence to reverse the recent past trends of the business, and the desire to shape their future. They wanted to find a new way to think about strategy and how to execute it. Doshi wanted me to return in another two months. I agreed, provided that, in the interim, the team could think through just one question: Is the office of the future going to be like the office of the past?

The next chapter of the book will attempt to provide new methodologies to formulate strategy, when industry definitions are blurring and when rapid change brings both opportunities and threats to a business.

Summary

- Many companies think of developing new strategies for their business only when they are in trouble. But successful and stable periods might indeed be a better time.

- All strategy exercises should be an attempt to keep the business relevant in the future, to address the next needs and wants of its various stakeholders, over a period which could be short, like two years, or somewhat longer, like five years or more.
- Many data-driven analytical techniques to formulate strategy are taught in B-schools, peddled by consultants, and practised by businesses. The limitation is that they bring one to the present expecting them to then extrapolate the future. Unfortunately, since the future is rarely like the past, there are major errors in assumptions. This often results in strategy failure and resultant frustration.
- There are two major strategic reasons why these exercises have limited usefulness in today's business environment: (i) the difficulty in defining the industry one is in; and (ii) the change around us and, even more importantly, the ever-rising rate of change.
- Change is everywhere, in different aspects of our life, and affecting the world of business in multiple ways as well. Changes are also happening very fast. Just think of the impact of demographics, urbanisation, renewable energy, connectivity, online shopping, search engines, artificial intelligence, social media, the gig economy, cable and streaming, and so on. The other aspect of change is the interdependencies among such changes. Take online shopping, for example. This form of doing business needs access to computers or mobile devices, the availability of the internet, Wi-Fi services, the development of web design and services, high-speed broadband, improved productivity of home delivery services, and access to credit cards. Without all of them, the business model does not form a closed loop.
- There will be three different, but mutually interactive changes that will lead to value creation in business. It can be conceived as a cycle of change vectors that will influence

and trigger change in the other two vectors when one is changed. These three are: consumer needs priority change; new technology and inventions; and business design innovations. Thinking around them, understanding them and sensing their interdependencies is key.

9

Strategy

Creating Transformational Strategies

Returning for a bit to my first meeting with Dilip Doshi at the London Business School. He had said, 'Professor, we are in real trouble … the competition is killing us.' This is a prevalent belief, and a refrain that we academics and consultants hear often. I told him, 'The reality is that it is *customer choice*, not the competition that is at the root of your problems.'

Feeling troubled by declining profits is often the mother that gives birth to a new round of strategy work in a company. When the work starts, the focus and data gathering is all about the current industry one operates in and the current competitors one has, especially the more successful ones. The speed at which the strategy work is finished is equally important, as one must be seen to be taking action during troubled times. Any action is good enough. Most of the time, the outcomes of such exercises predictably do not deliver – but it buys time; a year or two of new activities to pursue – and then the cycle starts again, often with a new set of leaders and players.

Beginnings of a Transformative Strategy

This work starts from a completely different place and with a completely different mindset. The business is prospering and does not have an immediate problem. So why initiate new strategy work? This is because an effective and thinking CEO and the board of a company want the business to continue to be successful in the medium term and, hopefully, in the long term. And when the work starts, it does not and should not begin with attempts to create a strategy. That is because strategy building is not the first step, or indeed the second step. It is the third step – and that too, a response to the first two steps.

So, what are the first two steps? Most people would answer this with 'vision and mission'. These have become cliché terms, and there are numerous interpretations of what those two terms mean and how they may be expressed in a business context. In reading many such statements from multiple companies in multiple industries, I have become a firm non-believer in the use of these terms. I find that they are mostly feel-good statements, framed and hanged on office walls, which no one remembers or internalises, and so they rarely feature in decision-making processes. Most importantly, they are not statements from where a robust or transformational business strategy can emerge.

Based on my readings over the years, facing issues as a top manager, and from strategy consulting experience, my go-to expression is 'core purpose'. For me, this is the first and by far the most important task in transformative strategy development. I have been greatly influenced by the writings of Jim Collins and Jerry Porras of Stanford, and especially by their first book, *Built to Last*, published in 1994.[1] I have liberally borrowed from their thinking and their expressions, and applied them to multiple businesses in my professional management and consulting career.

First Step Is 'Core Purpose'

It is the Organization's reason to exist. It is an enduring identity that transcends product or market life cycles, technological breakthroughs, management fads, and

> individual leaders. It is internal inspiration – it does not have to be exciting for outsiders. The role of core purpose is to guide, not to differentiate.
>
> – Collins and Porras, *Built to Last*

It is much easier to understand such concepts by looking at real-life examples. So here are a few examples of core purposes:
- Merck: Preserve and save human life.
- Walmart: Give ordinary folks the chance to buy the same things as rich people.
- Nike: Experience the emotion of competition and winning.
- Southwest: Meet short-haul travel needs at fares competitive with road travel.
- Tesla: Accelerating the world's transition to sustainable energy.

One can see from such examples that these are enduring goals that companies will always strive for. These can last a generation or two, as indeed they have done. When working on a core purpose for one's business, one must remember that it is something that must outlive today's generation of leadership. The overarching goal that one sets must be capable of lasting twenty-five years or more, notwithstanding all the change and the rate of change around us. In that sense, it is important to state a recurring long-term goal for the business, rather than those that are being specifically targeted in the short to medium term.

It takes deep soul-searching and hours of thinking and discussion to write an attractive and sensible 'core purpose' for the business. But wordsmithing is, relatively, the easier part. The most difficult and critical aspect is to gain acceptance and consensus – first from the top management, and then progressively right down to the factory workers, sales force, entry-level accountants, human resource personnel, and so forth.

In any business, it is important for those who have articulated a core purpose to have a company-wide discussion – say, every two to three years – on whether their purpose is still relevant and continues to be valid, at least for the coming decade or so. Equally, all new entrants into the business, in every operation, must be exposed to the core purpose statement and their alignment gained.

Second Step Is 'Targeted Future'

It is a clearly articulated goal. It is clear, compelling, a unified focal point for effort. It is tangible, energizing, focused and engages people at all levels.
– Collins and Porras, Built to Last

While the core purpose is the ultimate and enduring ambition with which the company operates, the strategy is more of a direct response to the targeted future, while maintaining strong alignment with the core purpose. The targeted future is typically an achievement goal in a five- to ten-year time frame. It can, but must not, just articulate growth and financial objectives. The best of them tries and describes what position and image they are aspiring for, and the quantitative business numbers they wish to achieve in the short to medium term. Once again, it might be easier to understand the idea with the help of examples:

Walmart wrote, in 1990, 'Become a 125 billion company by the year 2000.'

They took a simple-looking but audacious business-size objective. At that time, in 1990, Walmart sales were US$25.8 billion – they were seeking to become almost six times larger, in a more competitive market, in the next ten years. Did they achieve it? Yes, they did, in 1998 – two years before their plan. And in the year 2000, their revenues were US$165 billion, with more than double the number of stores they had in 1990.[2]

Now go back and look at their core purpose to give ordinary folks the chance to buy the same things as rich people, and targeted future. Once they had that clarity, designing a strategy (low prices every day, everywhere, and massive geographical expansion) to get to their goals became so much easier.

Here is another example of targeted future: Nike. In 1960, they wrote: 'Crush Adidas'. This was both a size-focused and competition-focused aspiration. But notice that they did not put down any numbers. Their single-minded objective was to defeat Adidas, no matter what size, spread and profit level they (as a competitor) got to. It was a moving target, based on the ideas, speed and activities of their key and more experienced competitor. Nike also had to be a far-out leader, where Adidas looked like an also-ran company.

Nike did achieve their dual goal (purpose: Experience the emotion of competition and winning; and targeted future: Crush Adidas). Though the rivalry continues to this day, Nike, with its US$37 billion revenue in 2020, is way ahead of Adidas at US$22 billion.

Look at Tesla. Their enduring goal is: Accelerating the world's transition to sustainable energy; and their more specific targeted future: 'We're building a world powered by solar energy, running on batteries, and transported by electric vehicles'. Launched in 2010, the company is currently expected to have sales over US$80 billion. In March 2022, Tesla hit a market capitalisation of US$1.1 trillion.

Third Step Is Defining Strategy

We have now reached the third step: What is strategy? In very simple terms, it is a 'logic' by which the corporate purpose and targeted future can be achieved. And what is transformative strategy? There is little difference; the answer is still the same. The difference is in the breadth and depth of ambition set down in the core purpose and the targeted future. In addition, the mindset with which one works is typically quite different. And, as mentioned earlier, one will fail to deliver a transformative strategy using the traditional data gathering and analytical processes, which focus on past data and current competition. We need to arm ourselves with non-idiosyncratic, new techniques, which give us a feel of the future and of what will work and remain relevant.

During my yearly part-time stint (for six years) as a visiting faculty at the Ross School of Business (Ann Arbor, Michigan), I renewed contact with Dr C.K. Prahalad, the celebrated strategy academic and university professor, with whom I had worked closely on a strategic project (Foresight) at Unilever. We taught during the same fall semester, and quickly became good friends. Over time, he also became my guide and mentor, as we spent many evenings together. One day, when tasting one of his favourite Brunello de Montalcino red wines at the Chop House Bar, he said, 'We can actually sense a lot of the future, if we listen to the soft signals, amplify them and connect the dots.' This became an inspiration and a building block for me to create a new methodology I shall discuss later in this chapter.

Many practising managers, management consultants and other experts believed for a long time, starting in the 1970s and going on even today, that strategy 'is a push to improve on all fronts and improve efficiency'.[3] To that end, many efforts were made and popular tags like total quality management, benchmarking, time-based competition, outsourcing, partnering, re-engineering and change management, to name a few, emerged and were widely practised by companies big and small.

But Porter saw the futility of somewhat mindlessly doing these exercises without having clarity on 'where you want to go, and where you want to reach'.[4] In his seminal works, he wrote, 'Such manner of competition produces absolute improvement for everyone, but generally no relative improvement for anyone. Competitors quickly imitate management techniques, new technologies, input improvements and superior ways to meet customer needs. Competition becomes a series of races down identical paths. The more benchmarking companies do, the more they look alike. The more rivals outsource, imitate improvements in quality, cycle times or supplier partnerships, strategies only converge. And despite all this frenetic activity and energy expended, no one can win.'[5]

5 Steps to Creating a Transformative Strategy

Step 1: Ambitious targets
The first step, as mentioned earlier, is to articulate a core purpose and a targeted future that will require a transformation of both its current business and its people. Bravery, but not rashness, is an essential ingredient. Bigness, audacity and confidence are all important. A can-do spirit, no matter how seemingly difficult the task ahead, is an operating behaviour. A timid target, which is essentially an extrapolation from the recent past, is a non-starter. If the 'solution' is already known, 'transformation' is unlikely to be achieved.

Step 2: Mindset change
- *Future customers*: A relentless focus on imagining the customer of the future – five years from now, ten years from now, fifteen years from now. The customer of today is not the customer of tomorrow. Being able to address this spatial difference is critical. We also need to think of all the touch points of consumer needs and wants, and how to address them.
- *Beyond current industry and players*: Because of our day jobs, one is accustomed to knowing about our current products and services, our present technology, and our business processes. We are also generally thinking of our current competitors, and how to take them on. All these

are futile. We must develop a mindset where we look well beyond our narrowly defined industry of today. We need to think about broader consumer benefit areas, and how to satisfy them better than what is being done today. Take, for example, an area like healthcare. Can we imagine what the key issues will be in twenty years' time? And can we start thinking of how to solve them?

- *Collaboration*: What are the ways by which we can satisfy many of our customer needs through collaboration? Just a few years ago, a restaurant owner could not take an order from, let alone serve a meal to, a customer sitting at home and not in his restaurant. Today, a well-organised home delivery service makes this easily possible. My generation has largely experienced an era when all resources required, and all knowledge and competencies needed, had to be reposed inside the company. That was our core strength and key to our differentiation and success. Anyone outside the business was a competitor and therefore a threat. Today's managers must learn how to leverage the skills and processes that reside outside our corporation. The new mindset must move away from continuously thinking competition to strongly seeking collaborations.
- *Learn to shed the past*: 'Imagine the future, and then fold it in into the present', C.K. Prahalad used to say. Instead of doing that, our closest attachments are to our factories, our products, our selling systems, our supply partners, our collection and payments systems, our capital base, and so on, and we wish that nothing will change, and all these current resources will enjoy a long life. Also, consider the skill bases and expertise of our current employees. If you want to take them into the future, you can only extrapolate. So if one wants to work on a transformative strategy, one must consciously learn to shed the past.

Step 3: Impact of 'societal change' in our chosen area
In recent times, the idea that society is greatly impacted and changed by technology was propounded by Alvin Toffler, in his runaway bestseller *Future Shock*, published in 1970. A noted futurist, he forecasted many of the things that we have seen happening in the last fifty years. Consumer attitudes, needs, priorities and behaviours change as they are impacted. There are other things that exist that determine the future. One of them is demography. Here, I have attempted to draw some inferences about the changes society will see or will have to grapple with because of demography.

- There are 3 billion people globally who were born between the years 2000 and 2020.[6] These people, who are between two and twenty-three years old today, will be twenty-three to forty-two years old in twenty years.
- By 2050, 65 per cent of the population of 10 billion will be urban, that is, living in cities.
- The population is ageing. In 2000, people above 60 globally were 605 million. In just 20 years (in 2020), these numbers have almost doubled to 1 billion. They will double again in 30 years (2050) to 2 billion.
- People now want to shop for everything online and have their purchases delivered to their home.
- Around the world, infectious diseases are declining; on the other hand, chronic morbidities (like diabetes, body pain, digestive issues, heart disease, lung problems, stress, mental ailments and cancer) are increasing.
- Now, look at your corporate purpose and targeted future statements, and try to assess what these changes mean and the opportunities they might spawn in one's chosen benefit area. Imagine for a moment that one's ambition for the future is in housing, healthcare, entertainment, education or food service. Every business will get touched. What enormous opportunities lie ahead, and simultaneously,

what big potential threats? We will analyse some of them later in this book.

Step 4: Technological trends
Science and its applications, the varieties of technologies that are at our disposal today, are at the heart and soul of our betterment and progress. The reason we can provide superior solutions, often at lower costs, or with greater value, is due to the relentless march of technology.

One needs to get an overall sense of technologies that are available today, not just in one's own industry but in the economy as a whole; and one also needs to scour and get a feel of new breakthrough technologies that are in the incubator at the moment, are probably being commercialised on a small scale, and will fully mature in the next ten to fifteen years and will have applications in multiple industries. Think next-generation power sources from solar or hydrogen energy, as an example.

One good thing about contemporary technologies is that, unlike in the past, they are open systems and not generally proprietary; access to them is easy and relatively good value. Access to the most valuable of them all, namely, the internet, for example, is that thanks to 5G, Wi-Fi and a simple smartphone, 6 billion ordinary people can read, write and communicate with each other, research and seek information, and order things and have them delivered to their homes. Many complex technologies have been truly democratised.

One good way for a layperson to understand the power of new technologies is to think of end products which are in everyday use today at home, or in business, but were not available just twenty years ago. The ubiquitous smartphone of today was launched by Apple for the first time in 2007 – just fifteen years ago. Take Google for an example. It went public in 2004 – less than twenty years ago; today, there are 228 million Google searches every hour of the day. The first YouTube video was uploaded in 2005. Does anybody know how many videos are on it today? You can get everything: from lectures in biochemistry by Nobel laureates to the evergreen songs of Kishore Kumar.

Scientists had long attempted to sequence the human genome. That finally happened in 2003. One can see its impact on disease treatment, molecular medicine and various other biosystems. Bluetooth can now wirelessly connect so many gadgets; it came into being only in 1999. Driverless cars went beyond concept in 2012, when Google announced that it had clocked 300,000 accident-free miles of driving. 3D printing with open-source software development has produced spare parts, bionic limbs and even whole houses. Stem cells and gene editing, again, are of recent origin. Stem cells have been shown to become any type of cells in the body and can grow and repair organs like the liver, lungs, and so on. Gene editing, discovered by scientists in 2012, can alter an organism's DNA, and thus be used as a treatment for eradicating many diseases.

Imagine the broad array of technologies sitting under each of these spectacular product offerings which have changed our life for the better in the last two decades. There is a huge potential to apply and use many of these known and commercialised technologies among new industries and business applications.

A systematic search of which available and emerging technologies can be applied to one's business ambition is critical to design and implement offerings in the chosen space. This creates approaches of doing things in a way that no one else has done thus far, creating the key resource for innovation, and consequent differentiation.

Step 5: Business system innovation
This is the fifth and the last step of the three linkages that result in achieving transformation. Business systems are the systems and processes through which a firm operates. They also provide linkages and interdependencies between multiple activities that are performed in different parts of the business. So these produce quality in each stream, and then link and optimise the

whole system. In simple terms, they are the rules by which the business works.

Traditionally, and mostly true even today, business systems tend to be focused on the internal aspects of work at companies. Supplier selection, procurement processes, credit and payment systems, manufacturing lines, logistics, distribution, sales, and so on. There is a constant search to improve efficiencies and reduce costs. Often, they are small incremental changes, but nevertheless can have a large impact on bottom lines, given the volume and size of the business. There is much value to this approach and it is fully endorsed by us.

However, the real innovation comes when there is a holistic approach, and when avenues for collaboration, often external, are discovered.

Making a business system change to satisfy an opportunity that comes from societal trends can be rewarding. Here is an example. The largest online retailer, Amazon, found that online ordering was not suitable when the customer wanted to see the physical product, get the real feel of the texture, its styling, and a good and perfect fit. The obvious categories that would have real weakness in online sales would be things like clothing and shoes, to name just two. In response to these real customer problems, the company introduced a 'wardrobe' concept, wherein the customer could choose multiple products, or multiple sizes of the same product, or any combination of the two, and have them shipped to their home. Believe it or not, they made no payments for the shipment. They would then have a whole week to try out their purchases and decide which ones to keep and to return. The company would then bill and charge the customer's credit card for the items kept and offer free return shipping for those that they did not want. By making this system change, Amazon gained considerable sales of categories which had real intrinsic problems in the online space. In 2020, the company sold over US$40 billion in clothes and shoes; in 2023, it is estimated that revenues from these two categories will touch US$80 billion. An example which demonstrates what consumer insight and business system change can do for a business.

An even more impressive business system innovation that has completely changed the service standards and economics of an industry is in the case of restaurants. Traditionally, one ate restaurant food *at* restaurants. There was always a takeaway component, though. To get a takeaway, one had to telephone the restaurant, order from the menu, wait a significant period for the order to be ready, drive to the restaurant, pick up the food, pay for it and drive back home. Most of the time, the food had to be reheated at home before it could be served and eaten. And the taste of the reheated food was nothing like what one got at the restaurant!

Now see the changes in the environment. First, the demand for food ordered from an eating place, for delivery and consumption at home, generally at dinnertime, grew by leaps and bounds, due to a whole series of societal changes and technical enablers. This trend got a further boost in the last three years with COVID-19, as work from home meant that lunch orders got added, and all of those, too, had to be delivered to people's homes.

Restaurants, as we used to know them, were brick-and-mortar spaces, in a busy, often expensive, location, consisting of large seating areas, with furniture and interior décor, an exclusive kitchen with a chef and cooks, waiters and service staff; not to forget bars and restrooms. Behind these were invisible operations like procurement of raw materials, food storage equipment, cooking lines, dishwashing, cleaning and hygiene services, and so on. It was a complex operation, characterised by high fixed costs, an uncertain customer flow with seasonality, up and down weekly revenues because of weekend peaks, and a staff characterised by high turnover, who therefore had to be continually trained. This resulted in high prices for the customer and slim margins for the owner.

Technical and business system changes have completely transformed how the task is now done. To take care of an online home delivery order, one does not need a physical restaurant at all. All they need is a website and a credit card authorisation from the customer. Supporting this virtual edifice are two collaborators: a third-party commercial kitchen, and a home delivery service from the kitchen location. The restaurant brand can specialise as a single-themed cuisine, like Indian, Chinese, Turkish, etc., or can be multi-themed, offering multi-cuisine food items on their menu. Or a single owner could offer multiple brands, each specialising in one type of food. All the online orders coming in are then directed to the single kitchen, which prepares and packs the food, and sends it out to the ordering customer. The restaurant owner now operates with no high fixed costs like rent for the premises, furniture and fixtures, expensive refrigerators and freezers. He does not have to deal with fickle manpower. Virtually all his costs have moved from fixed to variable. Even the kitchen could be a capital cost or just a bought-out service.

Transformational strategy development, or for that matter, any strategy development, needs data. Without data and objectivity, the outcome would be idiosyncratic, and therefore have limited or no chance of success. The same outcome (of limited or no success) is likely to happen if one only works with past data. Being rooted in the past hampers understanding, and therefore the ability to create relevance for a future, when there is so much change all around.

Future success requires that one has an objective basis on which to shape a business. Data is required. But how does one get data for the unknown? What we have tried to argue is that a lot of what is going to happen in the future is already known, either fully or in part. The likelihood of being able to create relevance for the future is by listening to and studying the 'soft signals' that exist around us today, and by then amplifying them.

Three Forces and Their Interactions Create Data for the Future

I had been thinking hard about change, especially those changes that would affect the world of business. Future, and the changes it inevitably brings, is a double-edged weapon – it spawns opportunities, but also threats. Every opportunity grasped by one is a threat for someone else. Could we list some of the most relevant ones and generate data to understand them?

On another evening, this time in the lounge of the Executive Training Centre of the Business School (where the faculty was served free wine), I presented my model to Professor Prahalad. This is what I told him: There are three powerful and interconnected forces, which are changing all the time; because they are interconnected, they are also impacting the other two. My core argument was that one needs to simultaneously study and understand three things that are happening around us:

- Societal change, which is a mass embodiment of where customers are going or want to go.
- Technology trends, not only within one's current sphere of business but also around multiple seemingly disconnected areas – especially those that are publicly available or traded – which though not apparent at the start could profoundly impact the value of what one wants to offer to the market.
- Business system innovation, which involves refinement and optimisation of systems and processes that the organisation has or accesses. These are different and more efficient ways to reach the consumer, source funds, speed the manufacturing lines, and so on. Delivering to the consumers' door is not a new activity. It was done at a local level by newspaper boys, milkmen, etc. At a global level, letters were the first to be delivered to each mailbox by the post office; then on a large scale, and at high speed, documents and small packages got to the home (or office) delivered by courier companies; then to books and music; other packaged and

non-perishable goods; and finally, freshly prepared food. This type of innovation and inevitable improvements over time are bound to have a profound impact in the future.

I told CK, 'The important thing is that any one change affects the other force. Technological changes result in new products and services, which in turn affect and shape societal acceptance, and to cope with these changes, business systems are improved. Most of the time, it is new technology that is the trigger. But conceptually, any of the three could initiate change. This cycle generates the data for us to investigate the likelihood of what can be successfully offered in the future which could not be done in the past.'

'Interesting' is the only word I got in response from CK. 'Let me think about it,' he said after a long pause. 'Why don't you try this out with one of your clients, and see if you can generate the data, and if the model works to produce some breakthrough opportunity?'

Ever since, I have been doing this with good outcomes – I shall present some of these cases in later chapters of this book. Actioning a breakthrough opportunity or fighting an existential threat requires transformation. Transformational strategy development is covered in more detail in the next chapter. Strategy, in simple terms, is responding to one's ambition, and in that process, creating a business model that is superior to what is readily available to one today.

Summary

- One often hears: the competition is killing us. Though this is the common refrain and belief, the reality is that consumer choice, not the competition, is the root cause of one's problems.
- Work on a transformative strategy ideally begins when things are going well, and the company is therefore able

to allow a mindset that focuses on medium-term or long-term viability and success. Sometimes, though, periods of extreme distress are a good starting point because only a significant step-change in strategy could save the business.
- The first step of transformational strategy building is, believe it or not, not a strategy exercise. It is an articulation of core purpose (the reason for being); and a targeted future (what we want to become in five to ten years). It can, but must not, just articulate growth and financial objectives. The best of them tries and describes what position and image they are aspiring for, and the quantitative business numbers they wish to achieve in the short to medium term. The strategy is the outcome of the response to the first two statements.
- There are five steps to creating a transformative strategy:
  1. Step 1 is ambitious targets. Bigness, audacity, and confidence are all important. A can-do spirit, no matter how seemingly difficult the task ahead, is an operating behaviour. A timid target, which is essentially an extrapolation from the recent past, is a non-starter. If the 'solution' is already known, 'transformation' is unlikely to be achieved.
  2. Step 2 is mindset change. We need to imagine how to serve customers of the future. Thinking beyond current industry, current competitors, current assets, current technology is a core requirement. We are going to increasingly try a collaborative rather than a competitive approach.
  3. Step 3 is measuring the impact of societal change. There is much data already around us that often semi-accurately predicts the shape of the future (e.g., demographics). The rate of population increase or decrease results in multiple opportunities – every business will get touched. Enormous opportunities lie ahead, but so do big potential threats.

4. Step 4 involves mapping technology trends. Science and its applications, the varieties of technologies that are at our disposal, are the heart and soul of our betterment and progress. The reason we can provide superior solutions, often at lower costs or of greater value, is the relentless march of technology. It is important to look for and understand changes/improvements in technology, not only in one's own industry but across industries, for solutions that could impact one's offerings. Think about new technology and changes in technology in one small equipment, such as the smartphone.

5. Step 5 is business system innovation. Business systems are the systems and processes through which a firm operates. They also provide linkages and interdependencies between multiple activities that are performed in different parts of the business. Think of transformations created in online selling and takeaway food by business system changes and enabling technologies.

- The Three Vectors (customer need priority changes; technology trends; and business system innovation) Model was created by the author while teaching his MBA classes, and later applied during his consulting practice in multiple countries. It demonstrates how to gather data that guides strategy development for the future.

10

Transformation

Ambition to Strategy

After reading the previous two chapters, the reader would have got a feel of the approach and the tools that I think work – we are now ready to give a description and shape to transformational strategy.

To recapitulate, strategy is responding to one's ambition, and in that process, creating a superior business model than what is available today. And transformational strategy is very much the same – the differences being only in the scale of one's ambition and an exponentially heightened ability to execute with both mind and heart.

Over the years, my learning came from education, followed by various multilevel experiences in Unilever businesses around the world; thereafter, from multi-industry strategy consulting assignments, and finally, in discussions with colleagues in business, students in MBA classes, and faculty in academia. All of these taken together contributed to my 'adoption' of certain ways to articulate complex ideas in simple terms to aid execution and action. In answering what strategy must deliver, I have been influenced by many, but most of all by Alan George Laffley, former CEO of Procter & Gamble, and Roger Martin, Dean of the the Rotman School of Management, and their book, *Playing to Win: How Strategy Really Works*.[1] The ideas explained below owe a lot to these two distinguished scholars.

Business strategy attempts to address and answer four (simple-sounding but complex) core questions:
1. Which customers are being targeted?
2. In which playing field?
3. What products, services and experiences do they need and want?
4. How is the company going to deliver and, more importantly, win?

The differential quality of a strategy, and its likelihood of success, depends heavily on the answer to the fourth question, which therefore is the most vital.

Let us begin by articulating an example of a 'transformational strategy'.

Case Study 1

Whenever I visit Mumbai, I stay at the Cricket Club of India (CCI). I was sitting there one afternoon, on the veranda facing the Brabourne Stadium, talking with Ramesh Sadarangani (name changed), owner of a medium-sized business in the housing sector. The company, started by his grandfather in Baroda in 1951, was expanded along traditional lines by his father and currently builds and sells apartments in Baroda, Surat and the Mumbai suburbs. It has a good reputation among its customers, the building trade and also good relationships with the local regulators. The third generation, Ramesh, in his early forties, is a civil engineer from IIT and an MBA from the MIT Sloan School.

Ramesh Sadarangani (RS from hereon), the new CEO, hero-worships Bill Gates and Paul Allen, who co-founded Microsoft. He is inspired by what Bill Gates had said in 1975, when they had started: 'Early on, Paul Allen and I set the goal of *a computer on every desk and in every home* [emphasis mine]. It was a bold idea and a lot of people thought we were out of our minds to imagine it was possible.'² Ramesh's dream was to enable every household in India to own a home.

We started working together. After much thinking and deliberation, spread over three months, across the whole company, RS announced the following:

Core purpose: Fulfilling the dream of every household to become homeowners.

Targeted future: Be regarded as an innovative builder, who 'democratised home ownership' in India. In five years, prove the concept and build at least twenty-five apartment buildings in five cities in three regions; in ten years, build 500 apartment buildings in seventy-five cities across India.

The company has stated which consumers they are targeting. They have identified their playing field (seventy-five cities across India). They know their offering (apartment homes). They have thus answered three of the four strategy questions. Now comes the most interesting, creative and difficult part of the exercise. The actual strategy to deliver and win.

Validation of core purpose

Before starting, RS needed to validate whether their core purpose and targeted future were consistent with demand trends of the future. And the evidence was positive. In India, in 2020, there were 280 million households (95 million urban), in a total population of 1.4 billion. In twenty years, in 2040, these numbers are projected to grow to 320 million households, with urban households at around 130 million (40 per cent). This is going to be a growing market, with demand rising for 40 million new households, of which 35 million – almost the total requirement – would be in urban India.³

In 2020, 30 million households in urban India did not own a home and were renting. Add to this the 35 million new homes that will have to be made available to meet the demand in the next twenty years. So the total market of households 'dreaming' of becoming homeowners is potentially 65 million – a very large opportunity for conversion of actual and potential renters into homeowners. So market-size potential was not a problem. The task was to find the conditions that would make home-ownership, which is universally desired, a practical reality.

The reason why households are unable to fulfil their dream of owning a home is predominantly financial. Even a small two-bedroom apartment is prohibitively expensive in most places. Second, the developing but conservative, and sometimes unimaginative, banking, and other lending systems rely on traditional databases, wanting a large down payment coupled with high interest rates.

Analysis followed. To break this logjam, one conceptually needed four things: new technology, a significantly lower cost of construction, reduced time from foundation to handover, and a more imaginative mortgage methodology. These must be done on a commercial basis so that the 15 per cent to 20 per cent return on investment is maintained or improved.

Innovation in construction technology

The news is that there are major developments in construction technology. A future technology scan revealed new products that were getting commercialised and scaled up. Most promising among these were 3D-printed housing – also known as additive manufacturing – and modular construction.

What is happening to 3D-printed housing? Plans for building apartments have been approved by regulatory authorities in Germany. Peri, a German construction company, is assembling the structure using parts made by printers developed by a Danish firm. Projects are up and running in Austin, Texas, to Dubai, Saudi Arabia and Singapore. Dubai is dedicating a district to host 3D printing companies and their warehouses. By 2030, the Dubai government wants one in four of their new buildings to be 3D-printed. Similarly, Saudi Arabia intends to build over 1.5 million homes in the next ten years, using this technology. Even the Indian Ministry of Housing and Urban Affairs has expressed that it wants to develop 3D printing-based housing to address its shortages of supply versus demand.

Are there several companies operating with this technology, and how are they spread around the world? Will such products be available in India? Well, there are quite a few good companies building a track record and commercialising the technology. The well-known ones around the world include: Apis Cor in Russia, CyBe Construction in the Netherlands, WinSun in China, ICON in the US, BeMore 3D in Spain and WASP in Italy.

However, well-established internationally approved building codes remain a major challenge. The regulatory process is predictably lagging the swift expansion of the technology and its commercialisation. But its potential is so big that many local officials, like in the US and Germany, are approving these buildings, and international codes should emerge soon. The other emerging technology set to change the face of home construction is 'modular construction'. Though known since the 1940s, its history has been a series of ups and downs. Recent improvements in materials, design and software applications are giving a new surge to this old idea.

So what is modular construction? In broad terms, modular construction involves producing standardized components of a structure in an off-site factory, then assembling them on-site.[4] These homes can cost up to 50 per cent less compared to traditional 'on-site' construction methods and can be erected in less than half the time. This is a powerful proposition.

The other developing technology is software for architectural space planning. Here is an example: A typical two-bedroom, two-bathroom apartment in India averages around 800 square feet. In the project we are doing, the architects managed to design a consumer-preferred two-bedroom unit in 625 square feet – almost a 25 per cent saving in space requirement! It also contains inbuilt storage space up to 100 per cent more than currently available. Since apartments are sold on a per square foot basis, application of such design techniques brings down prices significantly, benefiting potential home buyers.

Solar panels and household wind turbines

Advancements in generating clean energy are very crucial for home construction projects. New-generation solar panels are going to adorn the roofs and other available spaces in new buildings. Recent advances in wind turbine technology have miniaturised wind energy generation to rooftops and road dividers. These are being used in Israel, among other countries. Not only do these provide clean energy, but the outputs of newer designs are also growing exponentially, thus being able to meet the power requirements of entire apartment buildings, with limited space usage. And these will become available at a fraction of the current costs of traditional electricity.

So, to summarise, four distinct technologies – 3D printing, modular construction, architectural space design, and solar and wind energy generation – when made to work together harmoniously, will totally transform apartment construction in terms of quality, cost and delivery times.

Experience of building in many markets around the globe has proven the viability of building in such a manner. But what is spectacular is that this approach, when implemented, results in 'half the cost in half the time'. That makes it superbly attractive. When RS learnt what all the above-mentioned technologies deliver, he realised that his capital investment would be halved and he could turn around his capital twice, doubling his profit cash flow. This is truly disruptive as the current industry norms get broken in all respects. Though delivering a superior modern product at 'half the cost, in half the time', the strategy work is nevertheless still incomplete. One big hurdle stands in front of us, which must be crossed to close the loop.

Mortgage issues

Our target group, the people who do not own their homes and are living on rent today, do not have the saving to buy a house outright, even though the cost of housing might be halved. They can, perhaps, make a small down payment at once, but will require to borrow the rest on affordable terms. This is where the model breaks down, as they cannot afford the terms of the current mortgage lenders in the market.

So a further innovation is needed, this time in terms of mortgages for homes. Long-term mortgages – fifteen years fixed, and thirty years fixed – are available to customers today. The way that industry works is that the interest rate, after taking all future trends and risks, is fixed; and the time, over which the capital and interest must be paid back, is also fixed. So, the variable becomes the EMI (equated monthly instalment). This is where many applicants get rejected, as they cannot demonstrate how they will pay that monthly recurring amount, and that too, over a long period of time.

The thinking cap was back on the heads of RS and his core team. The question was: how can we be sure that the prospective customer can pay a certain sum every month? The answer was: find something that they are already paying monthly. So we knew that their current monthly rent plus current monthly electric bill can be an assured basis. We also knew that they are used to typically paying a 10 per cent rent increase every two years, and an inflation-based increase on the electric bill.

In the mortgage model of today, there are three elements – two of them fixed (interest rate and time) and one variable (EMI). RS and team designed a model in which the two fixed elements would be the interest rate and EMI (current rent, current electric bill, and 10 per cent rent increase every two years); and the variable element would be the time in which the amount due is fully paid up. Thus, the time the customer would take to clear the debt would be customised individually. It could be fifteen years, twenty years, twenty-five years, thirty years, thirty-five years for the customers, depending on how the two other fixed elements panned out.

Initially, this concept caused some consternation. We were used to collecting variable sums per month from various customers, depending on the final ticket price, provided the time was fixed. Were we going to take a greater risk if the period was variable and unique for each prospective customer? Was it not risky to keep exposure beyond thirty years?

The new mortgage model is perhaps less risky for a few reasons. First, the monthly instalment value is proven to be affordable, as it represents current cost on rent and electricity incurred by the borrower. Second, defaults, if any, tend to take place earlier in the borrowing cycle, rather than later. This is because income tends to increase over time, based on longer experience, promotions, and so on. Third, the cut-off of thirty years is based on the antiquated notion of retirement at age sixty. With rising lifespans and better health, the earning years in one's lifetime are on a rise rather than decline. Fourth, by the later years, additional earnings from more family members, like children and their spouses, also accrue. RS and his team felt increasingly confident that the proposed mortgage system could work. They started to talk with some well-established lenders.

The elements of strategy described here in brief were then written up in detail.

On completion of the strategy work, I like to play an (intellectual) game with the client company. I encourage them to express the entire strategy in thirty words. There is individual and collective horror every time. But soon, they always manage to do it. This ensures clarity of thinking, ease of understanding, acceptance by all, and easy communication up and down the ladder, across the organisation. That leads to easy implementation.

Let us restate our core purpose and targeted future for Sadarangani's business:

Core purpose: Fulfilling the dream of every household to become homeowners.

Targeted future: Be regarded as an innovative builder who 'democratised home ownership' in India. In five years, prove the concept and build at least twenty-five apartment buildings in five cities in three southern regions; in ten years, build 500 apartment buildings in seventy-five cities across India.

In response to these ambitions, this is the strategy in thirty words:

'Target renters in urban with high-quality, significantly low-priced, quick move-in apartments, with low-cost electricity, paying mortgage with current rents, enabled through multiple modern technologies and financial imagination.'

Does the overall strategy and the thirty-word strategy answer the four strategy questions presented above?

- *Which customers are being targeted?* Households living in rented apartments today. They do not own a home today but are always dreaming of getting one.
- *In which playing field?* Urban locations. Initially in one region then in the whole of India. In the future, it could move to neighbouring countries.
- *With what products and services?* Affordable homes with modern construction and low electricity costs – to convert renters into homeowners.
- *How is the company going to win?* By offering prospective customers significantly lower prices per square foot, low electricity cost, access to online maintenance services, mortgage financed by current out-of-pocket rent and electric bills.

Is this strategy transformational? There is an undisputable consumer need and want that is waiting to be fulfilled. But no one has made an offer to address it thus far. But this company, by a combination of technological breakthroughs within the construction industry, other emerging technologies in energy generation and changing constants in mortgage determination, has created a 'new business model' that is superior to anything in the market today.

I think that this business, if it implements the strategy well, will do something truly transformational. I hope that you, the readers, agree.

Case Study 2

I have deliberately chosen this example from the same country and in the same housing market. The purpose of doing so is to demonstrate that within the same market, and in the same industry, one can formulate not only a different successful strategy but also a transformational one. I will also demonstrate that the two transformational strategies that emerged could do so because of the two different starting ambitions or core purposes.

Here is a successful builder who operates in the premium end of the market.

This story starts with a single consumer insight: 'When people buy a new home and move into it, they are not just moving homes – they are moving their lives.'

Core purpose: Fulfil the need to live, work, play and relax, all in a comfortable, safe neighbourhood.

Targeted future: Be regarded as an innovative builder who broke the silos between living, working, relaxing and playing locations into a single integrated neighbourhood. In five years, prove the concept and sell five buildings in urban India. In five more years, expand the idea with a combination of owned and franchised units.

Formulating the strategy work begins here. There is a lot of work ahead which must combine imagination and practicality, but above all, it must steadfastly respond to the ambition of the business (core purpose) and goals (targeted future). What is required are insights (consumer, societal, technological, business systems), thinking through the solutions to the opportunities ahead, and the constraints and blocks that may arise, and rigorous analysis. This multi-pronged approach will create a winning strategy.

Elements to build the strategy

While people who rent homes are dreaming of moving into an owned one, the actual process of buying one and moving into it is both exhilarating and agonising. There is no doubt that moving into a newly owned home is sheer bliss – it is an actual dream come true. On the other hand, the move, even when it is from one locality of a city to another (let alone from one city to another), is fraught with disruption in many aspects of our day-to-day physical and emotional living.

Can we find a convenient and practical way to lessen the disruption the customer faces, while also finding a revenue-generating business opportunity? The conventional thinking by builders, and by city planning, is to segregate localities by residential, commercial, recreational, manufacturing, transportation, and so on. While some of them, like factories, train stations and large bazaars can remain located as they are, a case can, and perhaps should, be made to think of consumer ease and convenience when it comes to living, working, shopping, playing, exercise and recreation in everyday life.

Second, cities are getting congested, and public transport quality is deteriorating. Going out to do anything, even simple chores, is time-consuming, expensive and oftentimes risky. How about providing basic services without people having to leave the residential premises?

Third, gated communities with some services are getting created, typically in the suburbs of big cities (Delhi, Mumbai, Bengaluru, Coimbatore, Hyderabad), generally with a horizontal layout on large tracts of cheap land. While there are some obvious advantages to this, there are problems, too, that restrict their appeal. The disadvantages are that they are often far from city centres and lacking in infrastructure like schools, colleges, medical services, shopping centres and office areas. As a result, they only attract retirees and the greying population.

Land availability in core urban areas is limited and rather expensive. So large horizontal spaces are not available. This is a core constraint that the business must acknowledge. The solution, therefore, is to go vertical.

Let us turn our attention to the starting insight that when people move homes, they are moving not only their home but their entire day-to-day lives. So, what are they leaving behind? A lot. People need a network of things and services which are located around them. They are typically standalone but close enough to access easily. When a person moves, he must find a new vegetable vendor, grocer, primary doctor, to name a few.

Let us try to list what all is left behind to understand what the customer will be looking for to create a new network of services near their new home.

- *Food:* Fruits and vegetables, grocery, snacks, ready-to-eat provisions.
- *Grooming:* Hair and beauty salon.
- *Maintenance:* Plumber, electrician, carpenter, handyman.
- *Childcare:* Crèche, daycare, playschool.
- *Elderly:* Home care.
- *Medical:* Primary physician, first-aid, emergency care.
- *Sports:* Facilities for badminton, tennis, pickleball, basketball hoops.
- *Exercise:* Fitness area, gym, walking path, cycling path, swimming pool.

- *Work:* Workstations, high-speed internet, meeting rooms.
- *Vehicle:* Routine service facilities, ordinary repairs.
- *Parking:* For cars, scooters/motorcycles; for visitors.
- *Security:* Watchmen, cameras and alarm systems.
- *Community:* Park, playground, clubhouses for indoor hobbies and gatherings, bars.

This is just an illustrative list and not a comprehensive one. The idea is to demonstrate that people who are relocating are leaving behind a lot of things, services and relationships, and need many more things in the new location than just a new home. They need a large variety of services and easy access to them is important from the point of view of convenience, time-saving, quality assurance and safety. They face much more disruption in their lives than is typically acknowledged. Also, in the last five years, especially, living and working spaces are coming under one roof. Working from home, at least for a fair part of the week, is becoming a rule rather than an exception.

Technology choice is critical for this strategy. While fulfilling customer need priorities is widely divergent between Case 1 and Case 2, that is not at all the case on the technology side. The four distinct technologies applied earlier, namely, 3D printing (additive manufacturing), modular construction, architectural space design, and solar and wind energy generation, come into play here too. To be a commercial success, all of these must be optimised, with the object of delivering solid engineering at 'half the cost in half the time'. Here too, these must be made to work together harmoniously, thus transforming apartment construction in terms of quality, cost and delivery times.

There is an emerging, but clear, opportunity arising to create a 'hybrid' of personal living space, commercial space and recreational – all under the same roof. This is thinking of and as a consumer, and not just as a builder.

The pillars on which the strategy must be built are starting to become visible. Here are the four questions that every business strategy solution must answer:

- *Which customers will the company serve?* The young, affluent, and well-to-do, with a working wife and small children, who wish to buy or rent an upmarket premium home in a large city, or in a suburb of a large city.
- *In which playing field?* Suburban areas of large urban cities in India.
- *With which products, services and experiences?* Modern, spacious, high-rise buildings offering living, working, shopping, playing, relaxing facilities, all under the same roof. New technologies in construction, architectural design and space planning, power generation and transmission, electronics for communication and security systems will be harmoniously brought together.
- *How will the company win?* First, by locating the facility close to a large urban centre. Second, by easing the disruption when people move homes – spaces providing modern, electronically savvy apartments for living, but alongside spaces providing a whole host of services that help it to become a self-contained infrastructure. One can live, work, play, relax, shop and socialise, all under the same roof. Third, by creating a community and a neighbourhood that is 'vertical' in construction but 'horizontal' in feel. Fourth, by providing cutting-edge construction technology, state-of-the-art, low-cost, uninterrupted power supply and advanced security systems. Fifth, by passing on to the customer the cost benefits of 'half the cost in half the time' construction. And finally, by giving them access to customised mortgage facilities.

This, in our opinion, is a truly transformational strategy created to respond to a big ambition. The business model expressed in answer to the question 'How will the company win?' is unique and is superior to anything available in the market today.

Many pages will express the full strategy for this business. But to be sure that it is a unique business model and is easily remembered and equally easily communicated across the organisation, one must be able to express it in thirty words.

Here is how the thirty-word strategy statement came out:

'Offer premium vertical neighbourhoods in urban India, where families can live, work, shop, play and relax under one roof, through deploying new technology in construction, clean energy, electronics, security and lending.'

Case Study 3

This is based on a real-life happening in a large, nationally present, fast-moving consumer goods (FMCG) company, headquartered in eastern India. The company had acquired a healthcare business a few years before this exercise started. It was run at the top by elderly folk, but the next generation was slowly taking over, and they were ambitious about growing the business to its full potential.

Pradeep Banerjee (PB) (name changed) smiled warmly as I walked into the Nagaraj Bar at the Bengal Club in Kolkata. 'We want you as a consultant to create a business plan to significantly grow our existing portfolio,' he said. My response was a little lukewarm. But as the evening wore on and the discussions progressed, we agreed that we should attempt to achieve something big in the healthcare space.

'Do you have a well-articulated core purpose?' I asked.

PB said, 'I do have one in my head; it is loose and woolly – but we do want to do one'.

I told him, 'You will need one if you want to work with me on a new strategy.' We agreed to start with an investigation of societal trends.

At the next meeting, this time in the company's boardroom, with a senior, multifunctional team, I asked at the start, 'So what societal trends do you think would impact healthcare in a big way?' Silence followed. But after some minutes, the group warmed up and many thoughts started pouring in. What everyone agreed on was that there was a new priority in consumer lives with health, food and fitness, and that they were closely interlinked. A working group was formed to research trends in all these three areas.

The team went to work. When I returned in three months, a long list was ready. We sifted through it and chose what seemed the most relevant:

- First, and perhaps what was game-changing, was that there was a distinct shift from 'communicable and infectious' diseases to 'non-communicable, lifestyle-related' diseases. Twenty years ago, two-thirds of disease incidences in India were infectious or contagious. In the current times, the ratio had reversed and two-thirds of adverse health incidences were chronic, lifestyle-related morbidities.[5]
- Second, food habits had changed, with fewer home meals and more out-of-home meals as compared to the past. Simultaneously, while people were busier, they had become more desk-bound and sedentary in their habits, with exercise and physical activity taking a back seat.
- Third, there was a clear trend that people wished to be youthful, and desired to look so.
- And finally, people were more concerned with solutions than sticking to an ideology.

The company gathered nine major societal trends, of which the four explained above were the main forces.

At this juncture, let me mention that treating infectious and contagious diseases is very different from treating the chronic ailments prevalent today. Anyone can contract an infectious disease and the patient will realise that they are sick. A visit to an allopathic doctor, a short course of antibiotics, a few days of rest at home, and one is fit and ready to resume one's normal day-to-day activities.

Lifestyle disorders, however, are an adult problem – they afflict people above the age of thirty-five. Diseases like high blood pressure, diabetes, digestive problems, body pain and such creep up without the person realising that something is wrong and that it is going to get worse. The treatment with alternative and natural medicine tends to work better to manage such problems. These require ongoing, often lifelong treatment with medicines, alongside good food habits, exercise and good sleep. Despite this change in the nature of ailments affecting a large population, no one – be it the patients themselves, doctors or pharmaceutical companies – was offering a comprehensive solution to preventing lifestyle-related disorders.

Alongside these societal trends, the company did research with consumers around health, food and daily activities. The highlights from the research were:

(i) There are three broad situations related to health which are perceived differently from each other. 'Prevention' is a non-medicine, food- and exercise-related work. Then there is 'cure' for a '*beemari*' or illness, typically tackled through allopathic medicine. And lastly, there is 'treatment' for a long-term condition which will not go away, and therefore must be managed.

(ii) Health, or a concern relating to health, typically starts becoming an issue after the age of thirty-five. To the consumers' mind, being healthy is to be 'looking and feeling younger than your age'.

(iii) Unhealthy lifestyles create health problems. Consumers actively seek solutions and it is becoming common practice to combine allopathic with natural medicines, like taking oral medication for blood pressure, and traditional medicine for liver health.

(iv) Though desired, preventive measures are taken by a small minority; most people act on a health issue only when some 'trigger' pushes them to do so. The list of such insights was seventeen items long and explanations of them ran over scores of pages. With this work done, the company was ready to articulate their core purpose.

PB and his senior team went for two one-day off-site meetings and engaged with a professor from IIM Calcutta. They had a working model to discuss with me on my next trip. Here is the final version:

> *Core purpose:* Inspiring and enhancing the quality of human life by enabling people to feel better, remain youthful and enjoy an active life.

This met the ambition test. It was a large, inspiring and energising long-term goal that could take twenty to thirty years to realise. The people in the company felt that they were engaged in a noble job, benefiting the entire society. This purpose was presented by PB to the company board and was enthusiastically approved by them. They were keen to know what was going to happen next.

The team began to think about what future they wanted to target. There were many meetings and discussions across the company. The core team consisted of a multifunctional senior-to middle-management group, facilitated by me and a couple of strategy consultants. PB was the formal leader.

In a couple of months, they presented their 'targeted future':

> Be the pre-eminent player in the treatment and management of lifestyle-related disorders, pioneering collaborative and first-line treatment methods, with a INR 5,000 crore business in ten years.

This, too, was presented by the team to the board and was approved.

The company had to define which lifestyle-related conditions they were going to tackle, and the knowledge and technology

The six chronic pillars

Consumer research led to the insight that they were seeking solutions to six health conditions of a chronic nature. These were body pain (head, neck, shoulders, back, knee and overall muscular and skeletal systems); digestive (constipation, diarrhoea, bloating, gas, cramps); low vitality (energy, sleep, stress); diabetes (including pre-diabetes); heart-related (blood pressure, cholesterol, blood sugar); overweight. While consumers could suffer from any one of them, they often had more than one morbidity and significant numbers suffered from most of them.

Armed with societal trends and customer insights, PB and I put the next question on the table. 'What technology could provide a solution to mitigate these problem areas?' we asked. Allopathy was not the answer. Those chemical molecules did a good job curing disease but provided little medium-term effect in chronic disorders. Ongoing use of such medicines also resulted in severe side effects. Typically, one looks for technology in the pipeline, or in the future, to deal with the unsolvable problems of today. We need new science and new knowledge. However, in this case, the technology or medical system that could address the health problems of older people lay in the past and not in the future. Ancient Chinese medicine and Ayurveda provided the base knowledge. That was the science that the company had to harness. Products developed by in-house scientists had to be product-tested, and in some cases clinical trials needed to be done to establish proof of efficacy and safety.

PB and team started working on the 'building blocks' of strategy to meet our ambition and goals.

We had identified a transformational space – no company was an authority on the major lifestyle-related health disorders. The need was rising exponentially, but there were no players to systemically service these needs. It was also a phenomenon of the bigger cities, as pollution, rush, poor food habits and little exercise led to the inability of our bodies to cope and thus fall victim to elevated blood pressure, blood sugar, stress and other similar disorders.

The strategy had to first identify, and then eliminate, the blocks to deliver on this promise. Many people did not believe in natural treatments inherent in ancient Chinese and ancient Indian medicine. Proof of efficacy and safety had to be generated, and then provided. The quality of doctors dispensing such medicines was somewhat dubious too. One had to select a pool of doctors and give them credible certification.

One big strategic question was in respect of other medical systems, mainly allopathic: 'Are we going to be a parallel space? Are we going to show that we were better and compete with them?' The answer we reached was simple: 'We are not going to be confrontational. In practical fact, we would try our very best to collaborate. There was much to be potentially gained by collaborating with allopathic doctors, and much to lose, if we did not try and partner.'

First, the consumer trusted them; they were well spread out in large numbers; importantly, they realised that many of their patients had lifestyle-related disorders for which their usual prescriptions would not really work. So they might be half-willing to prescribe or verbally recommend traditional or natural medicines. They would, however, want to verify both efficacy and safety evidence, and it would be our job to provide that data. We defined such doctors as 'crossover' doctors.

The business model was taking shape. It had several customer value-creating elements that differentiated it from what was available in the market till then:
- First, no one offered a holistic solution to lifestyle-related disorders.
- Second, no other company in the natural products space had collaborated with allopathic doctors.

- Third, all medicines which were efficacious and safe would be available for acute and chronic conditions, for use both at home and outdoors.
- Fourth, the digital–physical platforms would give patients quick access to trustworthy doctors, while giving selected doctors access to new patients, without the need for a dispensary or travelling to homes.
- Fifth, the implementation would focus on thirty urban, high-potential markets, where lifestyle-related disorders were the most prevalent.

Altogether, this business model was superior to any other available in the market.

This transformative strategy was discussed thoroughly among the stakeholders and eventually written down. Predictably, it ran into several pages. But the question in PB's mind was: 'How do we get all the players, across all functions, across all levels, and across all geographies to internalise the strategy and plan their activities in a focused manner to achieve the goals?' The answer to that question led to the articulation of the strategy in just thirty-five words.

'Help 35-plus-year-olds manage various stages of lifestyle-related disorders through proven primary and complementary natural solutions via an ecosystem of modern and traditional doctors and trade to deliver advice and services conveniently.'

Truly transformational in its context.

Summary

- Strategy is responding to one's ambition, and in that process, creating a business model that is superior to what is available today. And transformational strategy is the same, the only difference being in the scale of one's ambition and an exponentially heightened ability to execute.

- Business strategy attempts to address and answer four simple-sounding, but complex, core questions:
  1. Which customers are being targeted?
  2. In which playing field?
  3. What products, services and experiences do they need and want?
  4. How is the company going to deliver and, more importantly, win?

  The fourth question and its answer are by far the most important.

- Three real-life case studies, all from India, demonstrate the process of the approach and methodology to be used to create a transformational strategy. Starting with core purpose definition and targeted future determination, the strategy is created using insight into customer wants, application of current and future technologies for better quality and costs, and new business systems. These practical applications are meant to show how the concepts are applied.

- Strategy is a consequence – it responds to the demands of the core purpose of the business and its targeted future. The full chain of expressing all three (core purpose, targeted future and the consequent strategy) takes space. It is, therefore, very useful to summarise the resultant strategy in thirty words or less. When done, it not only shows its core simplicity but its ability to be easily communicated to the rank and file, who must implement it in an aligned fashion.

11

Assumptions

How to Challenge Industry Assumptions

While insight, opportunity identification, restless energy, passion and ambition are the sources for articulating a core purpose, the ability to challenge long-held industry assumptions is at the root of transformational strategy creation.

Throughout the book we have argued for the need to listen to data and signals, sometimes even weak ones, that give one a feel of what is in the pipeline for business to deploy in an actionable way in the near-term future.

Second, we have established that this type of data gathering, though seemingly softer in content than hard data collected from the past, might be more beneficial for future strategy creation because, in simple terms, the future is not a linear trend line from the past onward.

Third, we have said that the data is sought under the heads of (i) changes in customer need priority; (ii) technological trends, not only in our own industry but all around us; and (iii) business system innovation. Together, they produce a rich data bank one can rely on to perceive and apply knowledge that others are not even aware of, let alone act upon.

All this data-gathering has a purpose. It provides the knowledge, feel and ammunition to start challenging currently held industry assumptions, thus finding a path to create differentiation and disruption. Mature industries and their key players become static over time. Their eyes do not look out any more; the ears do not hear. The marketplace becomes known and so do the technology and operating systems. Customers seem satisfied with the offerings. Players look at each other as sole competitors, and benchmark against each other to identify and implement marginal improvements to gain small temporary gains, generally in the product sphere.

Conventional wisdom says that there are five dimensions across which business strategy must be expressed:
- Industry assumptions
- Strategic focus of the business
- Customers
- Assets and capabilities
- Products and services

There is nothing wrong with sticking to these. However, conventional wisdom also takes into account:
- *Industry assumptions*: These refer to pre-existing conditions that are beyond an individual's control.
- *Strategic focus*: Build advantage by beating the present-day competition.
- *Customers*: Focus on the differences among them; the classic action is segmentation.
- *Assets and capabilities*: Leverage them as they represent the capital expenditure decisions made in the past, and the costs on skill development and training.
- *Products and services*: These are determined by industry boundaries of technology and knowledge.

This is very much the way 'industry analysis' and 'competition analyses' were framed from the 1970s onward. Added to this some time later was the theory of 'core competence'. All of them were somewhat inward-looking and static.

This is the way business strategy is taught, and this is also the way we learn to implement it in most companies. The problem with this approach, however, is that the outcomes are just incremental – most of the conditions are fixed and given, and the variables one can play with are restricted mainly to the product area. Much time and energy get spent in achieving small incremental improvements, which often escape the consumer's attention entirely. That is why large R&D departments with product focus deliver little real value or longevity.

Value-creating Methodology

Fortunately, there is a value-creating methodology based on the same five dimensions of strategy. The fundamental difference between the new and old approaches is the mindset with which one articulates them. The traditional approach, when armed with consumer insights, societal changes and technological trends of the future, is ready to move from static to the dynamic. One rarely obsesses over current competitors or looks into the rear-view mirror. We instead shift focus onto the future and on bringing about strategic change that can create new profit flows.

This is what the value-creating approach looks like:
- *Industry assumptions*: Conditions can be shaped; indeed, they must be challenged and shaped.
- *Strategic focus*: Current competitors are not the benchmark. Customer value is.
- *Customers*: Target masses; focus on key commonalities.
- *Assets and capabilities*: Not constrained by sunk costs; asks what needs to be done.
- *Products and services:* Seek solution to customer needs.

So this is the theory by which one works: use societal changes, technology trends and business system innovations, along with the right mindset, to be able to challenge industry assumptions on the five dimensions of strategy, and thus create breakthrough or transformational strategies.

From Theory to Practice

How does one apply this theory in practice? I offer three examples. I was deeply involved in creating the first product, Fair & Lovely. In the second case, I was a young manager in the detergents (washing powders) group in HLL, a victim of someone else's – Nirma's – breakthrough strategy. And the third is the story of IKEA, the Swedish furniture company which created a successful worldwide business in an industry which was always believed to be local in nature, and whose products were mostly always custom-made.

The story of Fair & Lovely (launched in 1975, almost fifty years ago)

Dimensions	Industry Norms	New Paradigm
Industry Assumptions	– Short-value cosmetics – Little emotional connect	Combine look of a cosmetic with performance of a medicine
Strategic Focus	Ponds and Colgate are key competitors	All women who wish to have a fairer complexion
Customers	Fulfilling skincare needs of mature women	Teenage girls; young, unmarried working women
Assets and Capabilities	– Low product technology – Glass packaging – Perfume	– Proprietary, patented formulation – Demonstrated to work – Approved by dermatologists
Products and Services	Vanishing and cold creams	All-purpose day-and-night cream in tube packaging

For the first time in the early 1970s, young unmarried women (for the most part) in India started working outside their homes in large numbers. They started buying a lot of clothes, personal care items, lipsticks and cosmetics. A cursory study of matrimonial advertisements in the local newspapers showed that prospective grooms wanted fair-complexioned brides. In those days, HLL marketing managers spent a lot of time visiting markets, meeting and talking with grocery and cosmetic shop owners. We also did a lot of formal quantitative consumer research – but such conventional research did not capture conversations or extract the deep feelings of the market.

So during my field trips to all the four regions of the country, I started visiting some homes and talked one on one with teenage girls and young working women, and some young men. The insights I gained from these conversations reconfirmed what we had found to be the trend in matrimonial advertisements – that nearly every young girl desired a lighter complexion. An improvement by a shade or two was considered good enough, as that would boost both their self-confidence and marriage prospects. Second, there were no racial overtones – all Indians considered themselves dark – even the fairest of Punjabis in north India.

Qualitative research done by Hindustan Lever and Unilever indicated that in India of the time wanting to look fairer was a universal desire among women. There were similar wants in all societies – the fair-skinned people in Western countries desired a darker, tanned skin, and spent time sunning on beaches and buying suntan lotions. Similarly, Africans wanted straight hair, and were spending money on products and services. I saw a germ of a new large opportunity. But how were we to progress on this? For marketing managers of that era, the cutting-edge tools were the newly minted industry analysis, segmentation of markets, competition analysis and so forth – unfortunately, none of them were going to be useful to make progress on this consumer-led idea. There was no product, no existing market, no competitors.

Disrupting existing order

I realised that we had to work on 'disruption', though the term did not exist in business back then. Could science deliver a product with such a benefit? Though skin-darkening products existed (suntan lotions and sprays), the opposite did not. We were in search of a new breakthrough formulation.

Time, including weekends, was spent in R&D laboratories, talking to our skincare and haircare product scientists on the possibility of a formulation that could make the human skin look fairer. And in that process, I discovered Dr Girish Mathur, principally a haircare scientist, who had invented a formulation in his quest to promote hair growth on the human scalp. Though he had failed to deliver on his goal of growing hair, he believed that the same formulation could prove useful in producing a fairer complexion in six weeks' time. Clinical trials followed and were conducted at a large hospital in Bombay. And we got our answer: it worked. The skin looked visibly fairer after six weeks of daily usage. The active ingredient in the patented formulation was a natural vitamin-based chemical – efficacious and with no side effects. The battle was almost won. A new formulation was our differentiator and disruptor!

I realised that first and foremost, a brand name had to be coined: Fair & Lovely was a good descriptor of what the product did, as the consumer had no past reference point. This was critical for establishing a new niche, and hopefully, in the future, a mass market. Second, we had to communicate that the cream was a perfect mix of cosmetic and medicinal – this would be our unique selling point. Third, efficacy had to be physically and visually communicated. Fourth, there could be no doubts about its safety.

The basis of our advertising story, created by Gerson da Cunha, then head of Lintas, was that the cream was good for the skin, apart from any other benefits. Here was a cream enriched with a vitamin that lightened the skin so it could revert to its natural tint, minus the tanning effects of sun exposure; Fair & Lovely was not a bleaching agent – it lightened the skin through a natural process.

The walls of the house

The market test proposal defined the walls of this new house:
- A descriptive name saying exactly what it did.
- Packaging design (tube and carton), with silky rich colour schemes to make it feel cosmetic and medicinal at the same time.
- Communication that the product worked in six weeks (complexion change getting noticed and commented on by others).
- Safe to use due to natural ingredients and no harsh chemicals. The underlying promise was that this would lead to a better marriage, which later morphed into a better career, and still later into a better life.

Just before the test launch in Madras (now Chennai), Nihal Kaviratne, who had also worked on the project, threw a spanner in the works. He asked the team whether a company of HLL's repute should be promoting skin lightening. The resultant pause was ended with the conscionable argument that it was the consumer making the choice to get the complexion they wanted – whether tanned or fairer, we were not there to judge, we were merely catering to a demand we knew existed.

The rest is history. Fifty years on, the product is still alive, growing, and one of the company's majorly profitable offerings.

The company is still on the ball about societal trends and recently renamed the brand. I believe that Hindustan Unilever has done the right thing by agreeing to change the name and taking out all references to skin lightening. Some fifty years since its birth, society has progressed, and the brand has evolved beyond offering fairness of complexion into a more complex bundle of benefits. To be inclusive is important today. And Unilever stands with this.

The story of Nirma (launched in 1969)

In this case study, we at HLL were the victims of disruptive innovation coming from one of our competitors.

Emerging India

This story begins in the India of the early 1970s. Forty-five years after Independence, consumer spending was becoming a visible contributor to the national GDP. Two-income homes were emerging in significant numbers, with many young, educated women joining the white-collar workforce. Rising education, higher incomes, dreams of success and access to television together stoked the need to start using modern packaged products, like those apparently used by richer households in urban locations.

In the early 1970s, I was the product manager for Surf, which at that time was the undisputed market leader in washing powders and was seen by both consumers and the trade as a high-quality, almost-imported product. It was widely distributed, with a strong reach in small-town India, came in multiple pack sizes and was heavily advertised in mass media, including vernacular press, at fairs and festivals, and on local street media, like walls and hoardings. Most stores prominently displayed the brand. Launched in 1959, Surf had captured the imagination of the urban consumer in the washing products market and had grown at a fast rate in the previous decade to a sales volume of 25,000 tonnes. A market, till then characterised by soap tablets and bars for fabric washing, was seemingly converting to washing powders, and soaking and washing in buckets was being adopted in a big way. HLL had brought real product innovation into a traditional market and was justifiably proud of its achievement.

There were two competitors in this market: Sway manufactured by Swastik; and Magic manufactured by Tata's TOMCO. All the three brands – Surf, Sway and Magic – played the same game with rules set by the market leader, Surf. Their respective market shares were: HLL's 70 per cent, Swastik's 15 per cent and Tata's 10 per cent.

The following rules of the game were accepted by all washing powder marketers: First, they targeted higher-income, well-to-do urban households. A decade ago, these, like the rest of households, were using hard soaps for washing their clothes. The only difference was that instead of loose unbranded soaps sold by the kilo, they purchased a more premium quality packaged and branded product, like Sunlight. Since most of the country has hard water, soap products were quite inefficient for fabric washing and gave poor-quality results. So, with the availability of non-soapy detergent powders, like Surf, giving much superior wash results, there was uptrading by such customers.

Second, all players chose the same product formulation (20 per cent active detergent, 26 per cent sodium tripolyphosphate [STPP]), installed spray towers (using a lot of steam energy), produced a low bulk density (0.22), free-flowing powder, all of them blue in colour and packaged in expensive multi-laminate cartons. Third, they all followed a multi-tier distribution system to reach retailers. Finally, priced at around INR 20 per kilo, they all earned high margins.

Year to year, market and sales growth were high in percentage terms, and there was happiness all around. Contrary to the euphoria described above and believed to be true by the modern industry players, the reality was far different. The penetration of washing powders, even in urban households, was only moderate after a decade of aggressive marketing, given that every household was washing clothes and was therefore a potential customer. Exclusive penetration was almost zero – almost all households continued to buy washing soaps, and as part-time maids were widely available, they were still giving the soaps to them to do the daily washing.

The convenience value to the housewife which came from washing powders used in washing machines was not a factor in India then, as washing machines were not available. The housewife was therefore not putting any value to convenience. This resulted in extremely low consumption per user household, and the pricey detergent powder was used only to wash special and delicate garments, generally by the housewife herself.

The disruptor

In 1969, Karsanbhai Patel, a chemist at the Gujarat government's Department of Mining and Geology, based in Ahmedabad, entered the scene. He felt that he could offer a washing powder to everyday customers at an affordable price. He started manufacturing a low-active detergent and phosphate-free synthetic detergent powder, with cottage-sector practices (dry mixing), and began selling it locally, home to home, delivering it on his bicycle. The new yellow powder (the colour of hard soaps; fully differentiated from other washing powders, which were all blue) was priced at INR 6 per kg, at a time when HLL's Surf was priced at INR 20. He branded it 'Nirma' (after his daughter Nirupama, affectionately nicknamed Nirma).

Through this simple-looking act, Mr Patel broke many industry norms and started a revolution still remembered by many, especially those associated with the grocery trade.

Rules of the washing powder game broken by Nirma

Dimensions	Industry Norms	New Paradigm
Target Consumer	Higher-income, well-to-do households	Everyday households aspiring to use branded packaged products
Formulation	20 Actives/26 STPP	10 Actives/0 STPP
Manufacturing	- Spray tower - Low bulk density 0.22 - High steam usage - One or two big factories	- Dry mixing - High bulk density 0.8 - Low capital, low power - Many small factories
Usage Instructions	- High foam - Soaking - Lots of water for rinsing	- Low foam - Less water needed for rinsing
Packaging	High-cost laminated cartons	Low-cost plastic pouches
Distribution	Three-tiered; high cost	First on bicycle; later, directly to wholesalers in full truckloads
Price	INR 20 per kg	INR 6 per kg
Profitability	High margin; low volume	Low margin; high cash flow
Communications	Mass media advertising	Customer incentives; later, jingle on TV

The first and most important challenge to existing wisdom was that many middle-income households were ready to start moving from commodity buying to reliable, quality, branded and packaged products. However, the price had to be right. Affordability was a must. This had happened, or was happening, in many other categories as well. One of them was small pack sizes (paisa packets) of tea; the other was toilet soaps, like Lifebuoy; the third was shampoo brands like Shikakai.

So the societal insight was that perhaps the great majority of middle-income people would upgrade when offered a good balance of superior quality (compared to what they were using then) and affordability.

Mr Patel realised that led by Surf, all available washing powders, like Magic and Sway, were grossly overengineered. The expensive spray-drying technology had been imported from Europe, and the formulation, also fully adopted, was designed for washing machines, not manual or handwashing. Indians did not have the habit of soaking clothes – they did not own washing machines, and many did not even use a bucket. That made the expensive STPP (a chemical that prevented redeposition of dirt back onto the fabric in a washing machine), which was a quarter of the formulation cost, totally redundant.

Also, due to owning fewer clothes but living in larger joint families, many homes washed every day, with the used clothes often being sweaty but hardly soiled. Third, most of the daily clothing was white cotton undergarments, which had no issues of colours running. Formulations could be harsher. In any case, the switch was going to be from ordinary washing soap – which, because of the prevailing hard water supply in most of the country, was rather inefficient.

Mr Patel's formulation decision – half the active detergent and no sodium polyphosphates – was correct for the market context, and was the biggest challenge to the prevailing wisdom. The European formulations had not been modified for the Indian market by the multinational-led players.

This combination of formulation and manufacturing decisions allowed Nirma to price their product at one-third the prevailing price per kilo. They also cut distribution and overhead costs. And Mr Patel was prepared to work with much lower margins in the hope of high volumes.

The Nirma entry truly transformed the fabric washing market in India, as it created new value at three levels: the consumer, the technology and business systems. Because of its greater relevance across society, the washing powder market exploded, expanding from 25,000 metric tonnes to 300,000 metric tonnes in a decade. Nirma became the market leader, as it expanded from western India to all over the country. HLL's Surf fought hard and retained its sales volumes but suffered heavy losses in market share.

And while everybody in the erstwhile industry (especially HLL senior managers) thought that it was a major case of discount markets taking over, it was exactly the opposite. Many households had upgraded to better-quality results, paying 50 per cent more per kilo from hard soaps to a washing powder!

The story of IKEA (launched in Sweden 1943, almost eighty years ago)

Ingvar Kamprad started his furniture business in 1958. At that time, home furniture was custom-made for wealthy upper-class people typically living in large houses. There was also a hand-me-down tradition in which furniture got passed down from one generation to the next. So even when the younger people added new items, they tended to order furniture designs like those from the past for continuity of look, character and harmony.

Furniture-making practices

Furniture was made to last for a long time. The design was traditional, often rounded and carved. A lot of labour went into each piece. They looked somewhat bulky but were required to, as space was not a constraint in the home. The material used was often teak wood, and the furniture items were all very sturdy, as they had to be long-lasting enough to be bequeathed to their inheritors.

Furniture-making was a small business, typically single-family-owned. There were considerable skills in design and carpentry, and knowledge of materials resting with these families – especially in wood, leather and textiles. These, too, were most often passed down from fathers to sons. The skill base, ethos and values were no different from, say, carpet makers in Kashmir or Iran. Their small establishments were in a bazaar area in the downtown of the larger cities – a small customer area in the front of the store and a larger production and material storage area in the rear.

It took a long time for an order to be delivered. Wait times of four to six weeks were the norm. One paid an advance with the order, and the balance was paid on delivery. Prices tended to be high for the customer. For the furniture maker, margins were high (labour costs were not counted), but volumes were low.

There was no advertising. Reputations were created through word of mouth, and customers walked in mainly through referrals. Sometimes, one saw some in-store advertising, or endorsements from satisfied customers.

The disruptor

Kamprad, a young adult during the Second World War, must have seen and assimilated some major societal changes which together could transform this traditional cottage industry. The first of them was that young people started leaving their parental homes after they completed their education, and especially after they got married. Young couples were leaving traditional large homes to go live in affordable small apartments. They needed to furnish their first new homes, but most of the available furniture would not fit in the relatively small spaces of their apartments.

The second societal change after the war was the advent and popularity of the passenger car. The big, bulky luxury cars of the few rich families gave way to the demand from young people for small, compact, affordable cars, which started appearing in large numbers. This completely changed the mobility of young people, who could now easily drive to locations away from the centre of town or city limits.

These new societal trends at the level of people (leaving parental homes, living in small apartments) and technology (spread of apartment housing, engineering and manufacturing replacing handcrafting labour, compact and less expensive cars) were creating conditions for a transformation. Contemplating these societal changes and technology developments, a new business opportunity was created in the founder's head, with innovative processes and systems, which when applied to the furniture industry, would become a business model totally unrecognisable from the past.

In 1958, IKEA (formed in 1943 of his initials, Ingvar Kamprad, those of his farm, Elmtaryd, and of his village in Sweden, Agunnaryd), moved from a catalogue-based mail-order business in traded items of household goods, and launched its first store in Almhult. That was the start of what is recognised today as the world's largest furniture retailer, with 474 stores in 63 countries and sales of 42 billion euro.

The breakthrough

Kamprad challenged many norms of the furniture business. First, he targeted young couples moving into and furnishing their newly acquired, relatively small-size apartment homes. Until then, furniture was bought by wealthy upper-class people, living in large homes with lots of space. Second, he brought a sea change to furniture design. He visualised lightweight, sleek-looking but sturdy flat panels, which could be easily assembled at home. And they were going to be suitable for the apartments in which his target customers lived. To his mind, there was no room any more for the traditional bulky, hand-me-down pieces of furniture which were used by their parents' generation.

Third, he invented new technology. The panels were mass-produced in factories, giving considerable economies of scale. Packaged in flat boxes, they were easy to transport both from factories to their stores, and from the stores to customers' homes. People could literally carry the boxes home in their cars. In this process, skilled labour got replaced by manufacturing, bringing much savings of costs and time. No more waiting for months to receive the ordered furniture. One just picked up the panels from the store, took them home and assembled them themselves. One could have a whole apartment furnished in just a couple of days! Furniture had become affordable for young people, thus creating a whole new market that was competing with nothing else like itself.

Fourth, the stores selling the products were large warehouses, with ample free parking space, located on the outskirts of the town. Each item one wanted to consider was fully assembled and displayed. But when you went to the delivery area, you only got small flat boxes to carry home. The existing norms had been smashed again. No more small, dingy stores in crowded downtown areas, where only a few items could be displayed, and where parking nearby was almost impossible.

Fifth, it was all cash and carry. Customers paid for the purchase in full, right at the point of leaving the store. No more a system of advances and payments on delivery. Sixth, prices were much lower. Affordability was a big element in the decision-making process for young people with limited incomes and low savings. Furniture was now available on a budget. Kamprad's model was: low prices, high volumes and low margins. Just the opposite of the traditional furniture trade.

Seventh, he advertised in mass media, once again targeting young couples. With his earlier experience in catalogue-based selling, he introduced catalogues for furniture selling, which had never been done before. In 2000, the catalogue became available in both printed and digital versions. In its peak year, 2016, 200 million IKEA catalogues were distributed in sixty-nine different versions, in thirty-two languages and to more than fifty countries.

Ingvar Kamprad challenged many furniture industry norms of his day, and in the process, broke many rules of the game which everyone else had accepted, not only in his native Sweden, but all over the world. Thus, over time, as he expanded over half a century, into ninety-one new countries, he was still the innovator, and successfully repositioned the existing industry into those markets. To better understand this business strategy, it might be easier to see it schematically.

IKEA challenges furniture industry norms

Dimensions	Industry Norms	New Paradigm
Target Consumers	- Wealthy upper class - Hand-me-down tradition	Young couples furnishing first home
Design	- Traditional, sturdy - Long-lasting teak wood	Simple, contemporary knockdown kits
Manufacturing	Skilled labour-intensive, customised, teak wood, back of store	In factories, mass-produced, reliable, low-cost materials
Trade	Small, fragmented, cartels, downtown, no parking	Big warehouse stores, ample parking, outskirts, cash-and-carry
Profitability	High prices, high margin, low volume	Low prices, high volume, low margin
Advertising	Word of mouth, in-store	Mass media

It was a big risk to take. But it was backed by solidly positive societal changes and the rebuilding of Europe after the Second World War, and the advent of new technology in home building, automobiles and mass manufacturing.

Continuous innovation

Over the years, many new products and business system innovations followed. The company remained steadfastly customer-friendly. A few examples demonstrate this. When IKEA found that customers could not easily cart away what they had bought in their own cars due to lack of space, they introduced home delivery service for a small fee. When they found that significant numbers lacked do-it-yourself talents and were struggling to assemble the kits, they started an assembly service, again for a small fee, done by company-certified carpenters and assemblers. To help consumers visualise what a whole room would look like when furnished with their products, they designed concept kitchens, bedrooms and living rooms. Even a studio apartment or one- to two-bedroom apartments were put on display in all major stores. One of the highlights was the demonstration of floor space saved, while at the same time the apartments looked elegant and well furnished.

No one knows for sure what was going on in the entrepreneur's mind. And I have obviously retrofitted this story to make it compatible with our theory and demonstrate its robustness. But it may not be as far-fetched as some readers might think.

Many years after he started his business, Kamprad gave some interviews and spoke about how he was thinking in the early days. When asked by reporters about what he wanted to achieve, and what he wanted to do, he said the following: 'to create a better everyday life for many people' and 'we shall offer a wide range of home furnishing items, of good design and function, at prices so low that a majority of people can afford to buy them'.

Don't these sound like what we call the 'core purpose' and 'targeted future'?

But whichever way one thinks, this is a truly transformational strategy. And, like all great transformational strategies, it was inspired by a big, powerful ambition.

Summary

- The ability to challenge long-held industry assumptions is at the root of transformational strategy creation.
- There is need to listen to data and signals, sometimes even weak ones, that give one a feel of what is in the pipeline, for businesses to deploy in an actionable way for the future. This type of data, though seemingly softer in content than hard ones collected from the past, might be more beneficial for future strategy creation, because the future generally is not a linear trend line from the past.
- When data is sought for (i) changes in customer need priority; (ii) technological trends, not only in one's own industry, but all around us; and (iii) business system innovation, it produces synergistically rich content for action plans.
- This gathering of data is not mindless – it has a purpose. It provides the knowledge, feel and ammunition to start challenging currently held industry assumptions and thus find a path to create differentiation and disruption.
- There are five dimensions across which business strategy can be expressed: (i) industry assumptions; (ii) strategic focus of the business; (iii) customers; (iv) assets and capabilities; and (v) products and services. There is a conventional and a value-creating mindset with which these can be expressed better. The latter creates the path by which current industry assumptions can be challenged.

- Three examples – those of Fair & Lovely, Nirma and IKEA – demonstrate how the process was successfully applied, thereby creating new businesses worth millions. Each one of them was the outcome of an ambitious core purpose and a transformational strategy.

12

Reinvent or Perish

Three Examples

McKinsey did a recent study which showed that the average lifespan of companies fell from sixty-one years in 1958 to eighteen years in 2022. They forecast that just 25 per cent of the companies currently quoted on the S&P 500 will survive the next five years.[1]

At the turn of the century, the top ten companies worldwide by market capitalisation were:

1. General Electric
2. Microsoft
3. Exxon Mobil
4. Walmart
5. Citigroup
6. Pfizer
7. Intel
8. British Petroleum
9. Johnson & Johnson
10. Royal Dutch Shell

If one speculated as to what would happen to their presence on this list and to their respective rankings in a span of twenty years, surely a plausible answer would be that they would all, with a couple of exceptions perhaps, remain on the top 10 list, though their relative positions might change marginally.

In 2022, all but one fell off the list. Nine of these once-venerable companies were not on the top ten list any more. Only one, Microsoft, remained. Ranked at number three now, down one place from their number two ranking twenty years earlier, they are the only one to have successfully reinvented themselves.

It looks like companies that are immensely successful and reach the top of the charts lose their pre-eminent position, often in a relatively short period of time, giving way to others who are often not on the list at all. This happens because companies are unable to see the change around them and the impact those changes will have on their enterprise. When businesses get very large and widespread, complexity also gets them down. Part arrogance, part smugness, part excessive attention on short-term operational and shareholder needs, and so on.

The Top Ten in 2022

Rank	Company	Founded	Market Capitalisation ($ trillion)	Sales ($ billion)	Net Income ($ billion)
1	Apple	1976	2.65	378	100
2	Saudi Aramco	1933	2.33	346	88
3	Microsoft	1975	2.10	185	71
4	Alphabet (Google)	1998	1.54	257	76
5	Amazon	1994	1.42	470	33
6	Tesla	2003	0.90	54	5
7	Berkshire Hathaway	1839	0.64	276	90
8	NVIDIA	1993	0.46	27	10
9	Taiwan Semiconductors	1987	0.57	21	21
10	Meta Platforms	2004	0.45	118	39

Source: Wikipedia

The one thing to note when we see the top ten companies today is that they are all, for the most part, very young companies. Only Saudi Aramco and Berkshire Hathaway were born around or over a hundred years ago; the oldest among the other eight leaders, Microsoft, began in 1975 – just forty-five years ago, and so did Apple. Amazon, which debuted in 1994, is less than thirty years old.

On the other hand, one can list many well-known companies and brands in the US which are more than a hundred years old. These are Coca-Cola (1892), JCPenney (1902), UPS (1908), Boeing (1917), L.L. Bean (1912), Harley-Davidson (1903), Kraft Foods (1903), Kellogg's (1922), Equifax (1899), Target (1902).

In India, at the end of 2022, the rankings were as follows:

Rank	Company	Market Capitalisation ($ billion)
1	Tata Group	311
2	Reliance Industries	203
3	HDFC Bank	131
4	Infosys	78
5	ICICI Bank	75
6	Hindustan Unilever	73
7	State Bank of India	66
8	HDFC Corporation	61
9	Bharti Airtel	56
10	LIC	54

Source: Wikipedia

There is another interesting aspect of the top ten list. Nine out of the ten are Indian companies. Multinationals have made little headway in the country among the large-sized enterprises – they are represented by one lone company, Hindustan Unilever. Also, except for the State Bank of India and the LIC, there is no public sector enterprise on the list – all the other eight belong to the private sector.

There are many successful companies and brands today that were already operating in the country a century ago. The largest of them are:
1. Tata Group
2. Bennett, Coleman Co. (the Times Group)
3. Britannia Biscuits
4. Century Textiles
5. The Calcutta Electric Supply Co. (CESC)
6. Dabur
7. Godrej & Boyce
8. ITC
9. Kirloskar Brothers
10. Shalimar Paints

Unilever (the alma mater of both authors) started trading in India in 1888 (134 years ago) and started its first manufacturing unit in 1931. The legal entity Hindustan Lever was formed in 1956, when three operating Unilever companies amalgamated. The history of all these eleven companies (and more) is proof that it is possible to survive and be successful as a business entity in a period of over 100 years.

So the questions to ask are: Why do most companies succumb to adversity? And how do some companies spring back and reinvent themselves after bad times? These questions were asked of me by Dr Abhijit Sen, a childhood friend, well-known nuclear physicist and former dean of the Physical Research Laboratory (PRL), while we were sipping on premium Darjeeling tea, sitting on one of his spacious verandas at his farmhouse in Ahmedabad. 'The more interesting one for me is your second question,' I told him, and for the next two hours recounted the stories of the London Black Cab, Lipton India and Apple.

Few Win, Most Perish

Business history shows that the most successful companies in any era are often recent start-ups that seemingly blindside the established companies in an industry. Examples abound. History also shows that companies typically arrive, grow, prosper and then at some point, start failing and eventually become irrelevant. Is there an inevitability to this life cycle?

In earlier chapters I have given more examples of the former phenomenon in which companies have grasped opportunities that others did not see. But the true test is whether ongoing large companies and industry leaders, when faced with difficulty and failure, can create transformational strategies to overcome their problems and get back to success and prosperity. Fortunately, there are companies that have successfully turned around.

The Near-death and Rebirth of the London Black Cabs

The black cab, the red double-decker bus, and the red, blue and white circular logo design naming the tube stations, are three iconic symbols of London's public transportation system.

The first mechanically propelled taxicabs were licensed in 1897, but it was the Austin FX3, built by Carbodies of Coventry in 1948, that became the familiar London black cab. Despite being a state-authorised monopoly, the 'black cab' operated within strict rules and regulations and had to comply with stringent 'conditions of fitness', both stipulated by the Public Carriage Office. It was a favourite among Londoners. At its peak in 2010, there were 24,000-plus black cabs plying in Greater London.

Then came the launch of Uber in London in 2012. And everything changed. Many felt that the black cab would not survive this onslaught. When Uber entered the scene, customers got a welcome new experience. No more walking out to look for a taxi. No matter where you were, the cab would come to your exact location, most of time in less than five minutes. It was reserved for you alone, the identity of the driver was known, you knew the fare in advance, and it was charged to the credit card stored in the system. The navigation set-up in each car ensured optimal routing, and what was best of all – it was significantly cheaper than the black cab. Uber had redefined the rules of the game!

Within a couple of years from the launch of Uber in London, the black cab was headed for the ICU – it was going to live only in pictures, it seemed, as a part of history. The manufacturer, London Taxis International, went into bankruptcy after over fifty years of successful operations.

New strategy to save the black cab

But the black cab business survived. It was brought back to life by Geely, a China-based parts and assembly supplier (to the London Taxis International, the failed and bankrupted manufacturer) who paid just GBP 11.4 million for the company.

Geely employed a transformational three-pronged strategy to save the London black cab. My imaginary thirty-word articulation of their strategy is: 'First, nullify the advantages that Uber has. Second, exploit all the inbuilt strengths that the black cab has over Uber.'

The Uber app, and the software technology that runs the application, is at the core of what 'disrupted' the conventional taxi trade. It is, on the one hand, very powerful, but surprisingly easy to copy, on the other. That is why Uber clones soon started appearing in all major markets of the globe. The GETT app, originally developed in Israel, came to London. You could now as easily order a black cab from your home, office, restaurant, or picnic spot. It arrived in less than five minutes, you knew the fare in advance, and could pay by credit card. And voilà! all the Uber advantages were gone.

Now, communicating the built-in advantages:
- *Easy availability* ensured that you could hail a cruising cab on the road or get one at a taxi stand (no Ubers available here; and no need for an app on a cell phone).
- *Spacious*, they can carry up to five to six passengers (Uber X can carry three, max).
- *Faster travel* to destination, as black cabs are permitted to use dedicated bus lanes (Ubers can't).
- *More luggage space*, including for wheelchairs and baby strollers.
- Better-trained, courteous and safe drivers.
- Sturdier, reliable and safer cars.
- Only a mild premium in fares versus Uber for all these benefits, and no surge pricing (unlike Uber).

The black cab nullified the benefits of Uber; but the Uber business model in turn could not nullify the state-given monopoly and other intrinsic benefits of the custom-made black cab. The black cab now had the upper hand. But the third, and perhaps the most important long-term strategic action, was the 'product redesign', at an investment of GBP 480 million.

Both authors now use only black cabs when in London.

The new cab

The retiring taxi is a 2.5-litre diesel, while the new LEVC TX has a 31-kWh battery and 1.5-litre petrol range extender. The new taxi has a range of 80 miles in pure electric driving, with the range extender giving an extension to 300 miles total. This taxi product is going to benefit all three stakeholders: passengers, drivers/operators and regulators. The passengers not only enjoy the familiarity of the old black cab, but also a great deal, more comfortable seating, and a lot smoother and noiseless ride. The panorama glass roof is a joy. Drivers have a modern car with all technological conveniences built in. Though more expensive to purchase, there are a lot of fuel costs to be saved in the medium term, and these cars are sturdily built to last fifteen to twenty years. The regulators, who banned new diesel engine cabs in 2018, have now had their prayers answered with a no-pollution model.

A promising future

Instead of vanishing and becoming history, the London black cabs are a 21,000-strong fleet today. And they are here to stay. Geely plans to sell 36,000 black cabs a year soon, not only in London, but also in Europe, and in many cities around the world.

A transformative strategy saved an icon.

The Rebirth of Lipton India

The story of Lipton began in the nineteenth century when Sir Thomas Lipton (1848–1931) of Glasgow, Scotland, opened a small store in 1871 to sell grocery items. While selling his varied products, he became fascinated with tea, a rare and expensive product in those days. He eventually bought his first tea plantation in Ceylon (now Sri Lanka) in 1890.

Lipton started trading in India in1898 and set up its first factory in Kolkata, among the first FMCG companies to start direct distribution from its factories to its stores. Company salesmen visited each outlet every week. Tea became one of the most widely available branded packs in India.

Unilever acquired Lipton globally in 1972. Lipton India Limited (LIL) was run independently of its larger sibling, HLL, and it retained most of its workers and staff, including all managers in leadership roles. LIL went public in 1977. Now the company had to publish the financial results for shareholders. That is when the shock came – the large, sprawling company with nationwide operations, and employing many hundreds of people in its factories and sales operations, was losing money. The share price dropped to below face value, causing immense embarrassment to Unilever.

Experienced business leaders from Unilever, HLL and LIL diagnosed that the direct distribution system employing company field force (2,000-plus numbers) needed correction. An indirect, but equally robust distribution system in terms of reach and service frequency, manned by third-party distributors working on a commission, and a direct sales force of just 250 people, was seen as a practical alternative and a solution to the problem. A crack team from HLL was deputed to install a modern, efficient and cost-effective one. It took three years, thousands of man-hours and exhausting travel by managers across urban and rural areas of the country to complete the herculean task.

There was some good news: sales management had done a great job and had appointed many distributors all over the country. But there was also bad news: the management had been unable to separate many of the unionised sales force. Costs, therefore, went up as stock distributor commissions on sales got added to the already bloated salesmen's wages – a double whammy, indeed.

Rajesh Bahadur, my boss during my Fair & Lovely days, then Chairman of Lipton and later Personnel Director of HLL, was most candid when he dropped into my visiting director's office, one day, on the fifth floor of Lever House. 'It was, in retrospect, both a wrong diagnosis of the problem and an incomplete implementation of a major plank. Sales management and Industrial Relations management should have worked together and created a plan that simultaneously appointed distributors while reducing the sales force. That unfortunately was not done. Thus, instead of reducing costs and creating efficiency, we had unwittingly ended by adding not only to costs but also to complexity,' he said.

Problems of superficial thinking and rush to implement

There was a strategic lesson to be learnt here. Superficial thinking and hasty analysis of a problem, and placing emphasis on implementing a half-baked plan, generally causes more problems than the ones inherited. Around this time, both the authors had been deputed to the LIL board, along with a few other HLL colleagues, to again attempt to turn around the business.

I was tasked with heading the domestic tea business. The first thing I decided was that there would be no short-termism, including declaring a quick return to profit. The new leadership team's analysis of the problem led to the conclusion that the company had not one or two, but many big problems requiring an all-round 360-degree effort. Beverages became a 'profit centre', with all operations under a single head, rather than the tea business being run functionally as 'the company'.

Four core issues were identified, abbreviated for this narrative as BQOP: Buying, Quality, Overstaffing and Product Portfolio.

There was no silver bullet. While the first two issues were more critical and had to be given higher priority, a steady state required that all four of them be resolved concurrently. Suboptimisations, a game often played in the past, had to be eschewed. A true 'transformation' of both the 'hard' side and the 'soft' side was the need of the day, and it was urgent.

It took a few months and many one-to-one and multi-functional group interactions among the leadership team to truly understand what the 'turnaround' required and to settle the strategy agenda. It was going to be both a 'mind' and a 'heart' game. Management at all levels had to know, understand, internalise and commit to the business objectives and strategy; then, they would have to figure out their functional roles and deliveries.

Buying

Quality and costs of tea approved for buying were the two biggest issues, and both heavily depended on how well the tasting, buying and blending functions were performed. At the time of intervention, considerable scope for improvement was found in each of these activities.

A unique complexity of the tea business is that the raw material varies with nature and season, unlike in the chemical or metals industry. A complex matrix emerges when a buyer plots the origin of the tea (Assam, Dooars, Nilgiris), the seasonality of each one and the quality parameters of aroma, and six leaf quality parameters. Three related but independent functions of tasting, buying and blending required different skill sets. Great tea quality may not be at the right price, whereas modest quality may well find a place in a particular formulation. After all, a target quality at a reasonable cost was the goal, as in any other business. Further, the teas had to reach blending and packing factories in the right quantity and at the right time.

Tea buying strategy and implementation had to be totally overhauled. The following steps were taken:

- Recognising that quality and quantity of seasonal supplies were inversely related, higher-quality teas had to be bought seasonally, well above replacement requirements, and held as a 'quality reserve' for the lean season. This helped to lower costs and quality consistency of blends.
- A five-year data analysis revealed that quite unintentionally, the company was buying teas in rising markets. The company switched to buying teas in falling markets; the exception was the higher-quality teas.
- The infrastructure of buyers, brokers and warehouses was rich in Kolkata, and less endowed in some smaller, though important, source centres (like Guwahati). The company moved its best buyers to those locations and significantly expanded the supplies from there.
- To reduce use of working capital, better planning and coordination among sales, production planning and warehouses cut the finished goods inventory, releasing much-needed working capital.

- The business-authorised purchase and lease of high-powered computers of that era to optimise these and other processes.
- Eighty per cent of tea blends were generated by computers. The blenders in the factories formulated the final 20 per cent to match the final quality standard.
- The people side in the buying and blending function was also transformed. As we have repeatedly said in the book, the two must go together and complement each other to achieve success.

Apart from these big steps, there were several other steps taken to streamline the supply chain from raw materials to finished products. Our team was relieved by some early success. It was cash positive and could declare a profit in the short term. While the short term had been successful, the company did not yet have a holistic solution. After all, two low-hanging fruits (buying, quality) had been addressed, but not the other two (excess manpower and brand portfolio).

The people issues

The industrial relations situation was tricky. There were excess workers in both the factories and in the field, and they were unionised. Cutting manpower in the 1980s was a pipe dream. Voluntary separation schemes, following regulatory guidelines, were toothless and no one budged. The team started building a proposal that would be attractive, humane and affordable.

The team sat down and developed seven insights:
- The first of them was that the cost to the company for each employee was virtually double of his take-home pay.
- Second, the employee felt secure about his household expenses only with the take-home amount.
- Third, people below fifty had greater family expense obligations relating to their children.

- Fourth, lump sum payments were more likely to be wasted due to imprudent expenditure.
- Fifth, monthly payments made into the wives' bank accounts had a greater chance of protecting the family from financial distress.
- Sixth, young employees could still find some full-time or part-time additional income avenues.
- Seventh, the unions had less of a say when the negotiations were one to one, and if done by the operating management rather than the central industrial relations department.

Armed with these insights, a holistic scheme was offered to employees through one-to-one meetings. Naturally, each employee evaluated the scheme from his own perspective and got the opportunity to discuss and understand the details better. Thanks to meticulous planning and strategising, it turned out that it was an offer that no one could refuse – a win-win for all concerned. Over 90 per cent of all employees approached accepted – they were grateful and appreciative. Another big battle to health and well-being for the business had been won. At a later time, a similar approach was successfully implemented in the major factories without any strikes or lockouts.

Brand portfolio

Now came the fourth strategic agenda, about the weak brand portfolio. Loose tea, the largest segment of the market, offered 'freshness', but because of seasonal produce, the quality went up and down, and so did prices. Packaged tea, on the other hand, could offer reliable year-round quality and more steady prices, but was seen to be not as fresh.

There would be considerable consumer 'value-add' if the two could be combined. This was the root insight that created the 'Taaza' brand – fresh tea that was packed close to the tea gardens and came to your hands within a month of manufacture. Until then, no brands of tea were as popular as the single blend sold nationally; each brand satisfied either the north or the south Indian market, in terms of taste and strength, but not both. For the first time, regional blends were offered inside the same outer packaging. All people liked the product they bought. In just two years, Taaza outsold the market leader.

Value addition to many functions

Four seemingly independent functions – Buying, Quality, People, Portfolio – melded together holistically with heart plus mind, and implementing both short- and long-term activities simultaneously gave the tea business of the company a successful transformation.

Apple: Near-death Experience and Reinvention

Today, Apple Inc. is the world's most successful company. It has a sales revenue of US$378 billion, a profit of US$100 billion, and a market capitalisation of about US$3 trillion.[2] Has it, however, always been this successful, with a string of successes one after another? No, that was not always the case.

Two men and a garage

On 1 April 1976, Apple Computer was born. Two young men, Steve Jobs and Steve Wozniak, launched Apple II, two years later. The company created its own proprietary designs and practised horizontal and vertical integration to become the most successful player in a nascent PC industry. By 1980, when it went public, it was selling over 100,000 units.

In 1981, IBM, Microsoft and Intel came together to completely change the competitive scenario. IBM did the PC hardware, Microsoft the software (the DOS operating system) and Intel the microprocessor (CPU). This across-the-board upgrade started steadily gaining market share and soon became an industry standard. More players entered the playing field by cloning the IBM PC. Cornered, Apple responded by launching the Macintosh (Mac) in 1984, which was more customer-friendly and more elegantly designed. But these 'cosmetic' changes could not hide its weak heart (low processor speed and inferior software), and earnings began to decline. Net income fell by 62 per cent between 1981 and 1984.[3] The approximately ten-year-old company was in a crisis, and Steve Jobs was forced to quit.

To explain the reinvention, I have relied on and referred to the Harvard Business School case study 'Apple Inc. in 2012' written by David Yoffie and Penelope Rossano.

The lost decade

The next ten years (1985–95) can be called the 'lost decade'. From a low, it rose with various short-term and predictable initiatives in the first five years, but then succumbed in the face of fast-growing competition and no real sustained differentiation. John Sculley, Michael Spindler and Gilbert Amelio were at the helm during this period.

Sculley expanded into desktop publishing and education and achieved some success with superior software and the launch of peripherals, like laser printers. He then presided over a series of bad moves like aping low-cost PCs, partnering with rival IBM to create a new PC OS, and working with Intel chips to raise processor speeds. None of them worked. Spindler took over in 1993. His three years were characterised by cost-cutting in the US, and growth programmes for overseas, but those did not reverse the losing trend, and Apple showed a loss of US$69 million in the first fiscal quarter of 1996. Amelio, appointed as the new leader, reversed course, and wanted to return to the earlier premium price strategy. But the company floundered, with more inward-looking initiatives, like job cuts and restructuring efforts. The net result was that the worldwide market share fell to 3 per cent, with a negative bottom line of US$2 billion. Many believed that Apple would soon go bankrupt.[4]

Steve Jobs returns

Steve Jobs returned to Apple and became the CEO again at the end of 1997. Thus began a new chapter in the history of the company – a period of twenty-five years until when the organisation was reinvented and rebuilt into its new avatar.

Arch-rival Microsoft saved Apple by giving Jobs a US$150 million infusion; they also agreed to develop MS Office for the Mac. Jobs restarted by refusing to license the Mac OS any more and stopped the licensing-to-manufacture programme. He appointed Tim Cook to streamline operations and the supply chain and expanded distribution from smaller outlets to national chains. Direct sales also began for the first time through a website. With the successful launch of the iMac in 1998, the company got back on its feet. Apple could post a profit of US$309 million in fiscal year 1998, reversing the US$1 billion loss in 1997.[5]

In earlier years, Steve Jobs had articulated his vision thus: 'My passion has been to build an enduring company where people were motivated to make great products. The products, not the profits, were the motivation.' Apple continued to innovate on premium-priced computers, but the first visible change to a new line of products started with the launch of the iPod in 2001. Music had become mobile since the 1950s, with the introduction of transistor radios, and became increasingly popular as those radios miniaturised. However, the sound quality was variable and poor, and nowhere a match to the home-based stereo systems. The breakthrough in marrying mobility with high sound quality came when Sony launched the Walkman, which sold 385 million units globally.

The iPod launch by Apple in 2001 was a quantum leap forward for the mobile music listening platform. It was also the first time that Apple moved beyond the Macintosh and computers from its product line-up. What was remarkable was that Steve Jobs did not invent any new technology to do this. He merely connected the dots between what was already available and synthesised. Jobs did three innovative things: first, he designed the beautiful iPod; second, he negotiated with the music industry the legal download of a music track; and third, he created the iTunes digital music software and store. For the first time, instead of carrying just one cassette tape or a CD, one could carry their entire music collection in their pocket. The iPod became an unparalleled success, selling 450 million units in its lifetime.

New core purpose in the new millennium

The iPod launch in 2001 signalled the change in Apple's core purpose, and the start of its new transformational strategy. For the first twenty-five years, Apple, in three phases, was just another ordinary company, with a not-unusual mix of success and failure. It had a successful first ten years, a floundering, near-death middle years, and then some years of reinvention, revival and growth.

There was a new purpose now, which stated: 'Apple's mission is to bring the best user experience to its customers through its innovative hardware, software and services.' In marking the company's twenty-fifth anniversary in 2001, Jobs said something to the effect that he saw many consumers were becoming entrenched in a digital lifestyle using phones, cameras, music players, camcorders, and so forth. Since that was going to expand exponentially, he wanted Apple to be the 'digital hub'.

Job's transformative strategy in fewer than thirty words (as imagined by the authors): 'The Mac will be the preferred hub to control, integrate and add value to all digital devices.'

The strategy consisted of four parts:
- *My customers*: the digital products/lifestyle adopters.
- *My playing field*: the digital universe of products, software and services; concentrate more on North America and Europe.

- *My products*: computers, phones, tablets, music players, streaming devices.
- *My services*: App Store, Apple music, iCloud, Apple Care, Apple Pay, Apple TV, Apple stores.
  How to win: by becoming the preferred 'hub' to control, integrate and add value; by control of both hardware and software; by superior design and presentation; by creating revenue-generating services; the Apple store where customers could experience the products and get repairs and expert advice; creating proprietary set of applications (Photos, iTunes).

Together, these changes created significant 'barriers to exit'.

Steve Jobs died of cancer on 5 October 2011. But the core purpose of the company he built was so strong and relevant, and the transformational strategy so sound, that they continue virtually unchanged until today. The new transformational strategy brought enormous and sustained growth to the business.

Summary

- In the year 2000, the top ten companies worldwide by market capitalisation were General Electric; Microsoft; Exxon Mobil; Walmart; Citigroup; Pfizer; Intel; British Petroleum; Johnson & Johnson; and Royal Dutch Shell. In 2023, none of them except for Microsoft has retained that status. All others were unable to remain contemporary or reinvent themselves.
- The top ten in India in 2000 were Wipro; Hindustan Unilever; Infosys; Reliance; ITC; ONGC; HCL; Pentamedia Graphics; Zee Entertainment; and MTNL. Here, only three of the top ten (Reliance, Infosys and Hindustan Unilever) have kept their place in the top 10 table.

- Both globally and in India, the largest and most successful companies could not cope with change and were also overwhelmed by the rate of change. Many of them were also obsessed with short-term goals, like quarterly earnings.
- Three examples – the reinvention stories of the London black cab, Lipton India and Apple – demonstrate how once-successful companies can lose their way, and how leadership and transformational strategies can reinvent them to find success again.
- The process of reinvention is the same. Look at societal changes, movements in customer needs priority, technology trends (both within and outside the current industry) and business system innovations. Use those to challenge industry assumptions. Collaborate. Use both the mind and the heart.

Epilogue

Adaptation Quotient of Future Leaders

As we near the end of this book, we reflect on how thinking and writing have been hard work, though joyous.

Hard work because our experience in writing a book together has been limited, though we have co-authored company business proposals earlier in our careers. Hard work because we reside on opposite sides of the globe, though, without doubt, we have been greatly facilitated by modern tools of communication. Hard work because our writing styles and approaches are inherently different, and we have had to find an imaginative way to harmonise our thoughts without harmonising who we individually are.

Joyous because we decided to concentrate on identifying the core themes that are intellectually precious to both of us and we placed a *cordon sanitaire* around those ideas. Joyous because we desperately wanted to be open-minded towards each other's ideas. This attempt tested our individual instincts of creativity, curiosity and discipline. Joyous because we felt, justifiably or otherwise, that we were pooling together perspectives and experiences gathered over a century for a novel manuscript, though we secretly hope that it may even border on distinctive.

Though we wrote one section each, we wrote on behalf of both of us, not individually. We must point out that the streams of thought in both sections are intimately intertwined. One section does not work without the other. In our professional lives, and in our various leadership roles, we have practised both the intellectual and conceptual sides simultaneously with people's engagement, communication and instilling individual commitment and collective motivation.

We are often asked, 'Which is more important – strategy creation or empathy skills?' Without annoying the questioner, we don't engage with this question. It is a bit like asking: 'Which is more important – the brain or the heart?' The natural ecosystems educate us on how it is a total system, wherein interfering with any one part can affect any or all the other parts. Hence, systems theory and principles are both relevant and a holistic approach is key to success. But nature informs us that there is one other aspect that is important – transformation is continuous and not episodic.

Nature's Lessons

We think it was just about thirty years ago that James Moore defined a 'business ecosystem' as a network of organisations and individuals that co-evolve. Relationships take many forms, for example, alliances, sharing intellectual property, data sharing, sharing human capabilities, so long as the ecosystem achieved benefits that no single partner could achieve by himself. Each of these books signalled a shift in thinking about business strategy: from the relatively static and linear relationship model articulated by Professor Michael Porter to a flexible concept of value 'networks'. By now, flexible, and adaptive supply chains and marketing networks are an essential part of strategic thinking.

The shift from 'models' to 'networks' implies resilience and adaptability.

A few years later, there were two seminal books, *The Death of Competition* by James Moore, and *Coopetition* by Adam Brandenburger and Barry Nalebuff. Their key insight, as understood by us, was that business relationships are not a zero-sum game. Relationships are a symbiotic partnership between players, built through cooperation, competition and innovation. Such a relationship wears out the unwanted tissues and creates new tissues for renewal.

Symbiosis is fostered through four methods, all derived from nature:

- *Diversity*: Biodiversity is a key element of nature. Organisations are far less inclined to encourage diversity of people, ideas, relationships and transformations.
- *Interdependency*: Ecosystem players are interdependent, and they behave in that manner whenever required. At the base of Australian eucalyptus trees there is often a hole. This hole is a 'marketplace for trade' – shelter for the possum in return for nutrients for the tree. Organisations' and leaders' mindsets have been nurtured on the maxim that 'winner takes all'. This was exemplified in the Nike hoarding at the 1996 Atlanta Olympics, 'You don't win silver, you lose gold'.
- *Adaptation*: Nature favours continual transformation, rather than episodic transformation. Animals and tress do not have a pre-designed 'transformation programme' at certain intervals. They keep adapting. Your body cells and skin are not what they were when you were in college. Why can't organisations see transformation as a continual activity without a start and a finish? That is one core challenge that our book tries to address.
- *Complementarity*: In nature, the biggest or fastest growing is not necessarily the most sought after. The most adaptive is the most sought after. That is why cockroaches and bacteria outlive the dodo and the dinosaurs. In *Small Giants* Jo Burlingham describes enterprises that chose not to grow to be what the founder wanted them to be – a great contributor to the community or a great innovator, where people worked for satisfaction and eudaemonia rather than for publicity and money!

Many things in life must go together, synergistically, with both effectiveness and efficiency. Actions must help the organism to stay alive and succeed. Organisations are like that, and so also the business transformation process.

The Practice of Leadership

At the end, this book is about the 'practice of leadership' in business. Businesses big or small, operating in one or multiple geographies, with narrow or broad offerings, with high volume or high margin, succeed or fail due to the quality of their leadership practice and its consistency.

We both went to Harvard Business School and did, at different times, the Advanced Management Program. We were exposed to and got to know various illustrious faculty members. One who made a big impact on us was Professor John Kotter, a leading expert on leadership.

While listening, talking and interacting with him, we became ardent followers of his articulation of the tasks that leaders should perform. His deeply perceptive yet simple-to-remember framework made a lasting impression on our young minds and helped our own individual practices of leadership at our respective organisations. According to Dr Kotter, the three tasks of a business leader are:

- Figure out what needs to be done.
- Accomplish the agenda.
- Ensure that the work is completed and properly done.

But these tasks are not unique to leaders; mid-level managers also need to do them.

What is unique about leaders is that they cope with the change, allowing managers to cope with the inevitable complexities arising from it. Leaders set direction – they design the vision and the high-level strategy; they do the aligning – fitting the right people to the vision and strategy; and finally, they motivate and provide inspiration so that the job gets done. What is noteworthy is that two of these three tasks relate to people, and only one to intellect and conceptual design skills. But they have equal weight when it comes to ensuring successful outcomes.

As Jim Collins, a Stanford professor, said, 'An effective leader catalyses commitment to and vigorous pursuit of a compelling vision and stimulates the group to high performance standards.'[1] In the two sections of our book, we have shared our learnings and experiences from our professional careers to put flesh and bones to these foundational ideas.

Transformation

Transformation is typically understood as profound change. In life, transformations take many forms: a caterpillar becomes a butterfly; a slab of stone becomes a sculpture. People are known to have transformed themselves from what they were to what they are now, and it could be for the better or worse.

But what does it mean in business? Transformation is coping with big changes, which could be both inside and outside the business. It might be required to grasp an opportunity in the future; or it could be initially defensive to correct past mistakes, and later aggressive to earn the right to thrive again. The Lipton and TISCO stories in the two sections of the book are good examples. Often, companies engage in organisational tinkering, pushed by either the CEO or the HR head, for trivial reasons or to cover up past mistakes, or just to buy time. Sometimes, single events need to be addressed, resulting in cost-cutting and layoffs. These would not qualify to be labelled as organisational transformation, though a lot of work and time is involved. It is only when one is addressing a big opportunity or countering a massive threat that one engages in real people transformation. In all such cases, structure follows strategy; never the other way around.

Amazon

Here is an example of a big transformation idea which is underway and will be visible to customers from 2024 onward. Four years ago, in April 2019, Amazon announced that the 'purpose' of a new unit in the company was 'to provide fast, reliable, affordable internet connection to unserved and underserved places around the world', meaning to every person on the earth. So have we not yet reached saturation levels in internet connections?

Sadly, the answer is no – we have 7 billion smartphones today, but only 5 billion are connected to the internet. The visible unserved market is 2 billion connections; add to it another 2 billion connections as the global population will soon touch 9 billion. Four billion new connections will be 80 per cent bigger (almost double) than the market of today! What are the reasons for not having a connection? Either a lack of network reach or poor affordability, or both.

Is this an ambition worth going after? Is Amazon's Project Kuiper practical? Is foundation technology commercialised to solve this? The answer is yes. Amazon invested US$10 billion into a constellation of 3,236 satellites that will remove both constraints – the uncovered geographies and the cost of a broadband, high-speed connection.[2] Much work still needs to be done, on both the business and the people sides, but this exemplifies truly transformational thinking. This is how next-generation businesses are created.

Training and Maturing as a Leader

The first quarter century of our lives is typically spent in an organised environment, in schools and colleges, learning language and grammar, science, mathematics, history, geography and so on. Also on the playing field, in a less organised way, we learn a variety of sports like football, cricket, badminton, tennis, swimming, and so on. Then, we live at home and develop our food habits, are guided by our parents on right and wrong and imbibe our value systems. These together form the core of our personality and character.

The next half century, we gain experience both as professional and family members, and these two together shape what we eventually become. Layers of knowledge bolstered by layers of experience mould to shape our effectiveness. This combination of the head and the heart is crucial to our business lives.

When the two of us look at ourselves and our professional careers, we feel that we started as 'archaeologists' and ended up as 'astronomers'. Archaeologists ask, 'What is inside this object?' Astronomers ask, 'What is this object a part of?'

Contrary to popular belief, these two professions have much in common, though, at another level, there are distinguishing differences. The common qualities are curiosity, a desire to listen and learn, analytical skills, problem-solving abilities, observation of detail and data interpretation, and being able to communicate effectively and collaborate. These are the foundational skills that remain forever.

However, in the first decade of one's career, one is closer to being an 'archaeologist'. Being a specialist in a narrow area, digging deep and developing a thorough understanding of the history and characteristics of one's industry, its customers, brands, technologies applied, competition, distribution systems for products and services, and so on. Having the energy and physical stamina for fieldwork, unflagging in hostile weather and geographic conditions, learning to manage both individuals and groups, while continuously imbibing the cultural climate of the company – but success comes only by applying these skills and experience.

In the next two decades or so, while retaining the common traits of both professions, one moves towards being more of an 'astronomer'. Starting to look up to the skies, the vast expanse of the universe, learning the identity of each in the planetary system, but also how they work together in unison. In a business context, industry gives way to society; from individual products and services to bundling experiences; from current specific science to future technology; from competition to collaboration. This is also the time to build on the initial people skills developed and start understanding the people around one as a total person, becoming trustworthy, a motivator and a counsellor.

At one time, one's head is soaring in the skies and at another, digging deep into the earth. As a leader, one must be an archaeologist, an astronomer – and a counsellor – all at the same time!

Abiding Philosophy

One last thought. There's a philosophy that both of us believe in, and following which has shaped us in a big way. 'Excellence is never an accident. It is always the result of high intention, sincere effort, and intelligent execution; it represents the wise choice of many alternatives – choice not chance determines your destiny.' These words are attributed to the Greek philosopher Aristotle, but as the authors of this book would vouch they ring true even 2,500 years later.

Acknowledgements

Thanks are due to

Krishan Chopra for being a persistent and motivating resource to the authors while doing this book—especially from Gopal: Krishan was the person who got him into writing by publishing his first book in 2007.

Jaishree Ram Mohan, Udyotna Kumar and Shyama Warner for doing a splendid job of editing, referencing and proofing the book—especially from Gopal, working with Jaishree for the second time.

Anil Ahuja for a splendid and imaginative cover design, which both authors appreciate.

Notes

CHAPTER 1   HEART PLUS MIND

1. *Vanderbilt: The Rise and Fall of an American Dynasty*, Anderson Cooper and Katherine Howe, HarperCollins, 2021.
2. John Gapper, 'Consultants Will Have the Last Laugh from the EY Fiasco', *Financial Times*, 16 June 2023.
3. Jeffrey L. Cruikshank and David B. Sicilia, *Engine that Could: Seventy-Five Years of Values-Driven Change at Cummins Engine Co.*, (Harvard Business Review Press, 1997)

CHAPTER 2   SOFTWARE: TRANSFORMATION AS ART

1. R. Kannan, *MGR: A Life*, Penguin, 2017.
2. Richard Rumelt, *The Crux*, Profile Books, 2022.
3. https://news.cornell.edu/stories/2016/07/frank-luck-looms-larger-success-most-us-think.
4. Michael E. Raynor, Mumtaz Ahmed and Andrew D. Henderson, 'Are "Great" Companies Just Lucky?', *Harvard Business Review*, April 2009. Available at: https://hbr.org/2009/04/are-great-companies-just-lucky.
5. Michael Betz, Joy Chen, Rock Khanna and Duncan Miller, 'Seven Principles for Achieving Transformational Growth', McKinsey & Company, 22 April 2021. Available at: https://www.mckinsey.com/capabilities/growth-marketing-and-sales/our-insights/seven-principles-for-achieving-transformational-growth.
6. R. Gopalakrishnan, *Six Lenses*, Rupa, 2015.
7. Rakesh Mohan (Ed.), *India Transformed*, Penguin, 2017.
8. Ibid.
9. ICMR, Case Study BSTR095, 2004. Available at: www.icmrindia.org.
10. Adam Grant, *Harvard Business Review*, March/April 2021.
11. Julia Dhar, 'How to Have Constructive Conversation' [video], TED, April 2021. Available at: https://www.youtube.com/watch?v=BFZtNN6eNvQ.
12. Bain Insights, 'The Company Cure for Initiative Overload', *Forbes*, 22 May 2014. Available at: https://www.forbes.com/sites/baininsights/2014/05/22/the-company-cure-for-initiative-overload/?sh=47d895f9413f.

13. Alex de Waal, 'New Pathogen, Old Politics', *Boston Review*, 3 April 2020. Available at: https://www.bostonreview.net/articles/alex-de-waal-thining-critically-pandemic/.

Chapter 3 Pain: Endurance and Inevitability

1. Torben B. Larsen, 'The Butterflies of the Nilgiri Mountains of Southern India (*Lepidoptera: Rhopalocera*)', *Journal of the Bombay Natural History Society*, 1987.
2. Ferris Jabr, 'How Does a Caterpillar Turn into a Butterfly?', *Scientific American*, 10 August 2012. Available at: https://www.scientificamerican.com/article/caterpillar-butterfly-metamorphosis-explainer/.
3. Louis V. Gerstner, Jr., *Who Says Elephants Can't Dance?* HarperCollins, Inc., 2002.
4. Russi Lala, *Creation of Wealth*, Penguin India, 2001.
5. R.H. Spector, 'Vietnam War', *Encyclopedia Britannica*, 30 September 2023. Available at: https://www.britannica.com/event/Vietnam-War.
6. Suresh Narayanan, 'Steadying the Ship amid the Maggi Storm', *Fortune India*, September 2018. Available at:/www.fortuneindia.com/people/suresh-narayanan-steadying-the-ship-amid-the-maggi-storm/102459.
7. Simon Sinek, *The Infinite Game*, Penguin Books, 2019.
8. Dorothy Kearns Goodwin, *Team of Rivals: The Political Genius of Abraham Lincoln*, Simon and Schuster, 2005.

Chapter 4 Leadership: Followers and Leaders

1. R. Gopalakrishnan, 'The Miyawaki Way to Grow Talent', *New Indian Express*, 18 May 2023. Available at: https://www.newindianexpress.com/opinions/2023/May/18/the-miyawaki-way-to-grow-talent-2576413.html.
2. George Anders, *The Rare Find: How Great Talent Stands Out*, Penguin Group, 2011.
3. Christopher Clarey, *The Master: The Brilliant Career of Roger Federer*, John Murray, 2021.
4. Gautam Mukunda, *Indispensable*, Harvard Business Review Press, 2012.
5. R. Gopalakrishnan, *Crash: Lessons from the Entry and Exit of CEOs*, Penguin Random House India, 2019.

Chapter 5 Review: Checks and Balances

1. Michael D. Watkins, 'Organizational Immunology (Part I: Culture and Change)', *Harvard Business Review*, 11 June 2007. Available at: https://hbr.org/2007/06/organizational-immunology-part-1.
2. Barbara Fredrickson, *Positivity*, Harmony Publishers, 2009.

Chapter 6 Long Life: Continual Renewal

1. Arie de Geuss, *The Living Company*, Long View Press, 1997.
2. R. Gopalakrishnan and Pallavi Mody, *How Anil Naik Built L&T's Remarkable Growth Trajectory*, Rupa, 2019.
3. C.K. Prahalad, *Fortune at the Bottom of the Pyramid*, Wharton School Publishing, 2005.
4. R. Gopalakrishnan and Sushmita Srivastava, *How Kiran Mazumdar-Shaw Fermented Biocon*, Rupa, 2019.
5. See, for example, Arindam Bhattacharya, Nikolaus Lang and Jim Hemerling, *Beyond Great: Nine Strategies for Thriving in an Era of Social Tension, Economic Nationalism and Technological Revolution*, Nicholas Brealey, 2021.
6. R. Edward Freeman, Jeffrey Harrison and Stelios Zyglidoupoulos, *Stakeholder Theory: Concepts and Strategies*, Cambridge University Press, 2018.
7. R. Gopalakrishnan and Tulsi Jayakumar, *How Uday Kotak Built a Valuable Indian Bank*, Rupa, 2021.

Chapter 7 Hindsight for Foresight

1. Statista.
2. Thomas L. Friedman, *The World Is Flat: A Brief History of the Twenty-first Century*, Farrar, Straus and Giroux, 2005.

Chapter 8 Future: How Much Will It Be Like the Past?

1. Statista.
2. Data given in this section is collected from the United States Census Bureau and other similar sources.
3. Andrew Ross Sorkin, 'What Will the World Be Like in 20 Years?' *New York Times*, November 2021.
4. US Energy Information Administration and the International Energy Association.
5. Statista 2023.
6. US Department of Commerce (Census Bureau News).
7. The Radicati Group, a technology market research firm: Email Statistics Report.
8. Statista.
9. Monica Anderson, Colleen McClain, Michelle Faverio and Risa Gelles-Watnick, 'The State of Gig Work in 2021', Pew Research Center, December 2021. Available at: https://www.pewresearch.org/internet/2021/12/08/the-state-of-gig-work-in-2021/
10. www.Netflix.com

Chapter 9 Strategy: Creating a Transformational One

1. James Charles Collins and Jerry I. Porras, *Built to Last: Successful Habits of Visionary Companies*, Century Business, 1994.
2. www.walmart.com
3. Michael E. Porter, 'What Is Strategy?' *Harvard Business Review*, November–December 1996.
4. Ibid.
5. Ibid.
6. United States Census Bureau.

Chapter 10 Transformation: Ambition to Strategy

1. Alan G. Lafley and Roger L. Martin, *Playing to Win: How Strategy Really Works*, Harvard Business Review Press, 2013.
2. Bill Gates at a news conference announcing plans for full-time philanthropy work and part-time Microsoft work, 15 June 2006, Redmond, Washington.
3. CEIC's economic databases – Census of India.
4. https://www.mckinsey.com/capabilities/operations/our-insights/modular-construction-from-projects-to-products
5. National Sample Survey Organisation (NSSO) data: 'Key Indicators of Social Consumption in India: Health, (2017-18)'.

Chapter 12 Reinvent or Perish: Three Examples

1. Quote from Dominic Barton, MD, McKinsey & Co, at the 2nd Economic Times Global Business Summit.
2. www.apple.com
3. David Yoffie and Penelope Rossano, Harvard Business School case study 'Apple Inc. in 2012'.
4. Ibid.
5. Ibid.

Epilogue

1. Jim Collins, *Good to Great: Why Some Companies Make the Leap and Others Don't*, HarperBusiness, 2001.
2. www.amazon.com

Index

Absorptive capacity, 58
Adaptability quotient (AQ), 30
Adaptation, 3–4, 31, 229
Adaptive layer, 92
Adidas, 152
Air India, 53
Akers, John, 82
Akzo Nobel, 51
Allen, Paul, 167
Alphabet (Google), 209
Amazon, 125, 139, 144–145, 159, 209, 210, 232
Amelio, Gilbert, 222
Anders, George, 79
Apple, 60, 209, 210, 221–225
Architectural space planning, 170–171
Art and science of transformation, 12–14
Artificial intelligence, 19
Assets and capabilities, 189, 190
Attrition, 77–78

Bahadur, Rajesh, 124, 216
Bajaj, 89
Banerjee, Ranjan, 124
Bargaining powers of suppliers and customers, 130–131
Barriers to transformation, breaking of, 114–115
Benchmarking competition, 131–132
Bentham, Jeremy, 99
Berkshire Hathaway, 209, 210
Bezos, Jeff, 125, 139
Bhabha, Homi, 13

The Big Con (Mariana Mazzucato and Rosie Collington), 58
Biocon, 103–104, 106, 109–110, 115, 116
Brahma mantra, for long-life companies, 94–97
Brandicourt, Olivier, 84
Brooke Bond India, 7–8, 65
Brooke Bond Lipton India Limited (BBLIL), 8, 24, 26–29
Buffett, Warren, 31
Built to Last (Jim Collins and Jerry Porras), 149, 150
Business design innovations, 144–145
Business institution, 100–104, 120
  giving back to society, 108–109
  people-oriented mindsets, 106–109
  shaping of, 104–106
Business partnerships model, 110
Business, practice of leadership in, 230–231
Business relationships, 228–229
Business strategy, 167, 189–190
Business system innovation, 158–161, 162–163
Business systems, 158
Business transformation, 2
  heart plus mind approach in, 4

Camp, Robert, 132
Canon, 132
Capacity for change, assessment of, 48–50
Carbon management strategy, 97
Cariappa, K.M., 72

Index

Catalogue-based selling, 203–204
CEO, 123
    choice and selection of, 78–82
    unfiltered CEO, 82–84
Change management, 3
Changes and rate of change, 135, 141–142
    connectivity, 137–138
    demographics, 136
    energy needs, 137
    gig economy, 140–141
    Google, 139
    interdependencies among changes, 142
    online shopping, 139
    social media, 139–140
    TV, cable and streaming, 141–142
    urbanisation, 136–137
    wireless devices, 138–139
Changes, mutually interactive, 142–143
    business design innovations, 144–145
    consumer needs priority change, 143
    new technology inventions, 143–144
Chidambaram, P., 33
Colgate Total, 143
Collaborations, 155
Collaborative competitors, 63–65
Collective legend, 22–24
    development of, 24–26
Collins, Jim, 231
Competitive rivalry, 130
Connectivity, 137–138
Construction technology, 169–171
Consumer research, 34
Continuous transformation, 14
Cook, Tim, 223
Coopetition (Adam Brandenburger and Barry Nalebuff), 228
Coopetition, successful, 64–65
Core competence, 189

Core purpose, 149–151, 168, 175, 183, 188, 225
Corporate Ayurveda, 97–100
Corporate immunity, 90
    adaptive layer and, 92
    innate layer and, 91–92
    physical layer and, 91
Cost control, 3
Cost leadership, 131
Crash (R. Gopalakrishnan), 83
Critical thinking, 101, 103, 105–106, 109–111
Culture, as innate layer, 91–92
Cummins Engine Company, 14
Customer of the future, 154
Customers, 189, 190
    bargaining powers of, 131
Cyclical learning, 113–114

Da Cunha, Gerson, 124, 193
Data, for strategy development, 161, 162, 188–189
Datta, Susim, 9, 32, 34, 124
Davie, Colin, 27, 28
Davis-Peccoud, Jenny, 53
The Death of Competition (James Moore), 228
Demographics, change in, 136
Demyelination, during transformations, 44–46
Dhar, Julia, 50
Dhulekar, R.V., 44
Differentiation, 131, 158
Directorate of Audio-Visual Publicity (DAVP), 11
Diversity, 229
Double-entry accounting, 98

Economic liberalisation, 8, 52, 100. *See also* Liberalisation
Effective organisation, 66
Efficient organisation, 66
Ekambaram, Shanti, 108
Emotional ownership, 105

Employee counselling by mentors, 78
Employee engagement, 91
Empowerment of people, 107
Engaged employees, 89, 91
Enron, 60
Ethnic/religious narcissism, 24
Eudaemonia, 119, 229

Facebook, 140
Fair & Lovely, 124, 191–195
Family planning campaign, 11–12
Farm bills, 63
Farming, 45–46
Federer, Roger, 79
Financial ownership and emotional ownership, 105
Ford Motor Company, 57
Forecasts, accurate, 125–126
Foreign currency convertible bonds, 110–111
Foreign Exchange Regulation Act (FERA), 32, 33
Foresight, 125
Foundations, for community service, 99
Fredrickson, Barbara, 92
Freeman, Edward, 116
Furniture business, 200–206
Future Shock (Alvin Toffler), 156

Gandhi, M.K., 25
Ganguly, Ashok, 80, 124
Gap, 59
Gapper, John, 3
Gates, Bill, 167
Gene editing, 158
General Electric, 58
General Motors, 57, 65
Gerstner, Lou, 82–83
Ghemawat, Pankaj, 42
Ghoshal, Sumantra, 33
Gig economy, 140–141
Glass, David, 125
Godrej, 89

Goodwin, Dorothy Kearns, 65
Google, 139, 157, 158
Grant, Adam, 50
Gupta, Shekhar, 65

Hagstrum, Jonathan, 46
Hanson Group, 51
HDFC, 82, 107, 110–111, 113–115
Heart plus mind approach, 4, 6, 7, 9, 12, 14, 221
Hershey's Chocolate Company, 23
Hindi, adoption of, 44–45
Hindustan Lever (HLL), 5, 8, 9, 32, 123–124, 192, 194, 195, 216
  acquisitions by, 36, 40
  collaborations by, 35–36
  counterintuitive strategies, 124
  innovation, emphasis on, 35
  liberalisation and, 32–37
  and Lipton India, 6–7
  organic growth of, 34–35, 37
  QICA efforts, 35–36
  quality drive by, 35
  sales reorganisation at, 5–6
Hindustan Unilever (HUL), 75, 78, 80, 82, 112, 210, 211
Human immune system, 90
Hussain, Ishaat, 81

IBM, 59–60, 82–83, 221
Ignite (programme), 107
IKEA, 200–206
Imaginal discs, 59, 60
  of social commitment, 60–61
Immelt, Jeff, 80
Imperial Chemical Industries (ICI), 51
Inattentional blindness, 50–52
Inclusiveness, 23
India, companies in, 210–211
Indian Civil Services (ICS), 70–71
Indian management talent, historical perspective, 70–72
ITC, 71

'India Shining' campaign, 53
Indispensable (Gautam Mukunda), 79
Industry analysis, 130–131, 189
Industry assumptions, 189, 190
Infosys, 78, 82
Initiative overload, 53
Innovation, 3, 131, 144–145, 158, 205–206
Institution
   business, 100–104
   definition of, 100
   for the people, 106–108
   shaping, 104–106
Institutional memory, 57
Intel, 221
Intellectual nomad, 24
Internet connections, 138
Irani, Jamshed, 20–22

Jobs, Steve, 221–225
Johnson, Samuel, 67
Joint stock company, 98
Jones, Reginald, 80

Kamprad, Ingvar, 200–206
Kaviratne, Nihal, 124, 194
Kelkar, P.K., 107
Kerkar, Ajit, 38
Kingfisher, 62
Knox, Andrew, 71, 72
Kodak, 57, 60
Kohli, Faqir Chand, 101–102, 106–107, 110
Kotak Education Foundation, 108
Kotak Mahindra Bank (KMB), 108, 111, 117, 119
Kotak, Uday, 108, 111, 115, 117, 119
Kotter, John, 53, 230
Krishnamachari, T.T., 45
Kuhn, Thomas, 102
Kurien, V., 26, 47–48

Laffley, Alan George, 166
Lall, J.M., 72

Larsen, Torben, 59
Larsen & Toubro (L&T), 104–106 111, 112, 117–118
Leadership development, in company, 73–75
Leadership Filtration System (LFS), 80
Lehman Brothers, 60
Levers of change, 118–119
Lever, William Hesketh, 99
Liberalisation, 8, 21
   evolution of, in India, 47
   and Hindustan Lever, 32–37
   and Tata, 38–43
LIC, 210
Lincoln, Abraham, 106
Lipton India, 6–7, 65, 215–221
Lipton, Thomas, 215
Listening, formal channels of, 28
Listening to signals, 46–47, 188
The Living Company (Arie de Geus), 97
London black cab, 212–215

Machine learning, 19
Mahindra, 78, 89
Mahuad, Jamil, 55
Malcolm Baldrige model, 41–42
Mallya, Vijay, 62
Management consultants, 58
Mandela, Nelson, 25
Marico, 107–108, 112–113, 116, 117, 118
Marico Innovation Foundation, 108
Mariwala, Harsh, 107, 112, 117, 118
Martinez, Arthur, 54–55
Martin, Roger, 166
Mathur, Girish, 193
Maugham, Somerset, 64
Mazumdar-Shaw, Kiran, 103, 108–110, 115
McKinsey, 31, 39, 82, 208

Mergers and acquisitions (M&A), 34, 36
Metamorphosis, 59
Meta Platforms, 209
Microsoft, 167, 209, 210, 221, 223
Miller, J. Irwin, 14
Mindset change, 112, 154–155
Mistry, Cyrus, 81
Miyawaki, Akira, 76
Miyawaki mini forest for talent, 75–78
Miyawaki technique, 76
Modular construction, 170
Mody, Minoo, 81
Monopolies and Restrictive Trade Practices (MRTP) Act, 39
Moonlighting, 140
Moore, James, 228
Mortgage model, 172–173
Motorola, 51
Mukunda, Gautam, 79–80

Naik, A.M., 103–105, 108, 112, 117, 118
Nair, R.R., 27, 28, 124
Naoroji, Dadabhai, 70
Narasimha Rao, P.V., 33
Narayanan, Suresh, 62
National Thermal Power Corporation (NTPC), 78
Nature
 lessons from, 58–61, 228–230
 metamorphosis in, 59
 on transformative adaptation, 3–4
Nestlé India, 62
Netflix, 59, 141
Newton, Isaac, 31
Ngram data, 3
Nihar, 112
Nike, 150, 152
Nirma, 195–200
Nurturing of talent, 78
NVIDIA, 209

Okuda, Hiroshi, 65

Online shopping, 139, 142
Operation Flood, 47
Optics, 62
Orbit shifting, 112–113
Organisation
 effective, 66
 efficient, 66
 going around in circles, 67–68
 key features of long-life companies, 95–07
 as part of bigger ecosystem, 95
 sustainable and responsible business practices, 98–99
 talent bench strength, 69–78
Organisational culture, embedded, 59, 60
Organisational transformation, 23, 44, 69, 86, 97, 114. *See also* Transformation
 pain of, 57–58

Paranjpe, Nitin, 2
Parekh, Deepak, 107, 110, 114–115
Parekh, Hasmukhbhai, 114
Parenting, 73–75
Participative model of leadership, 110
Past, understanding of, 123–126
Patankar, Vasant, 124
Patel, Karsanbhai, 197–200
People relations, 102–103
People Shield, 90, 92
Perceptions, 61–63
Phansalkar, Bhau, 124
Playing to Win: How Strategy Really Works (Alan George Laffley and Roger Martin), 166
Polman, Paul, 81
Porter, Michael, 130, 153, 228
Prahalad, C.K., 9, 12, 104, 153, 155, 162
Predecessors, blaming of, 87–88
Products and services, 189, 190
Progress diaries, 78

Index

Project Blue Chip, 118
Project Lakshya, 111
Purpose statement, 95–96

Rajadhakshya, Vasant, 5, 123–124
Ramachandran, M.G., 25
Ramadorai, S., 2, 42, 102, 107, 110
Recruitment density, 77, 78
Reinvention of companies
    Apple, 221–225
    Lipton India, 215–221
    London black cab, 212–215
Rejuvenation, corporate Ayurveda for, 97–100
Restaurant business, 160–161
RIDE (Recruitment, Induction, Development, Expansion) exercise, 76
Ripley, John, 9
Robber barons, 99
Royal Pigeon Racing Association and pigeons race, 46–47

Saldanha, Dicky, 6
Samuel, C.S., 65
Sanofi, 83
Sarin, Ramesh, 83
Satyam resolution, 64
Saudi Aramco, 209, 210
Schacht, Henry, 14
Scientific temper, 54
Sculley, John, 222
SCULPT mnemonic, 27
Sears, 54, 125
Self-digestive transformation process, 59–60
Sen, Abhijit, 211
Shapers' MBA, 100–101
Shastri, Lal Bahadur, 26, 47
SHE (sustainable, honest and enlightened) enterprises, 70
Sheth, Tarun, 124
Short term versus long term, 101, 103, 117–118

Sinek, Simon, 64
Singh, Manmohan, 33, 45, 114
Six Lenses (R. Gopalakrishnan), 32, 49–50
Small Giants (Jo Burlingham), 229
Smartphone, 134–135, 157, 232
Social causes, wealth for, 99, 108
Social media, 139–140
Societal change, 156–157, 162
Societal trends, 159, 180–181, 194, 202
Society building, role of business in, 119–120
Solar panels, 171
South Indian tea plantation industry, 51–52
Spindler, Michael, 222
Stakeholder orientation, 115–117
Start-ups, 100
    survival rate, 59
    things to do from beginning of, 102–103
State Bank of India, 82, 210
Stem cells, 158
Stepan Chemicals, 33
Strategic focus of business, 189, 190
Strategy development techniques, 130–133
    benchmarking competition, 131–132
    industry analysis, 130–131
    limited usefulness of, in today's world, 133–135
    SWOT analysis, 130
    war games, 132–133
Streaming, 141
Studer, Quint, 53
Subsonic echoes of transformation, listening to, 46–48
Suppliers, bargaining powers of, 130–131
Swaminathan Commission, 45
SWOT analysis, 130
Symbiosis, 229

Index

Tagore, Satyendranath, 72
Taiwan Semiconductors, 209
Talent bench strength, 69–78
Talent-building, 72–78
Talent filtration system, at Tata, 81
Talent management
   excellence in, 74
   induction in, 77
   journey of, 70–72
   recruitment in, 77
Talent planning and review, 75
Tandon, Prakash, 5, 71, 72, 80
Targeted future, 151–152, 168, 175, 183
Tata, 8, 89, 94, 99
   autonomy to group companies, 96
   collaborative and tolerant ecosystem at, 96
   conservative with financing, 97
   harmony with nature, 96–97
   joint venture with Burrough, 110
   liberalisation and, 38–43
   long-term vision and business model, 96
   purpose statement of, 95–96
Tata Business Excellence Model (TBEM), 41–43, 116
Tata Chemicals, 2
Tata Code of Conduct, 42, 43
Tata Consultancy Services (TCS), 2, 41, 42, 75, 81, 82, 101–102, 105–107, 110, 116
Tata, Dorabji, 60
Tata Group, 210, 211
Tata Group Innovation Forum, 43
Tata Innovista Award, 43
Tata, Jamsetji, 60, 99
Tata, J.R.D., 13, 20, 38, 60, 81
Tata Motors, 38
Tata Oil Mills Company (TOMCO), 36, 40
Tata Power, 96–97
Tata, Ratan, 8, 9, 38–41, 81

Tata Steel, 38, 42, 75, 78, 81
   corporate rationalisation in, 20–22
Technology, 3, 163, 178
   inventions, 143–144
   trends, 157–158, 162
Telecom industry in India, 62–63
Tesla, 150, 152, 209
Thomas, T., 80–81, 124
Threat of new entrants, 131
Threat of substitute products, 131
Tiffany, 59
Titan, 75, 81
Tobaccowala, A.H., 83
Toffler, Alvin, 156
Toyota, 65
Training courses, 78
Transformation, 23, 24, 228, 231
   adaptiveness of team in, 27
   art and science of, 12–14
   breaking barriers for, 114–115
   capacity for change, assessment of, 48–50
   on continual basis, 94, 229
   continuous, 14
   demyelination risk and, 44–46
   Heart plus mind hypothesis, 4, 6, 7, 9, 12, 14
   HR professional in, role of, 27–29
   inattentional blindness and, 50–52
   listening carefully in, 46–48
   luck in, role of, 29–32
   in nature, 59
   non-scientific temper and, 54–55
   and pain, 57–58, 61
   risks of, 43–55
   slow down to go faster and, 53–54
Transformational leadership, 4
   efficiency/effectiveness, 65–68
   going around in circles, 67–68
   holistic leadership approach, 20–22
   intellectual nomads, 25

and transactional management, distinction between, 19–22
Transformation management, 2–4, 10–12, 20, 69
    and transformational leadership, difference between, 19–22
Transformation programme, working of, 86–89
Transformative adaptation, nature on, 3–4
Transformative strategy
    development, 148–149
    core purpose in, 149–151
    defining strategy in, 152–154
    targeted future in, 151–152
Transformative strategy, steps for creating of, 154
    ambitious targets, 154
    business system innovation, 158–161
    case studies on, 167–186
    mapping technology trends, 157–158
    measuring impact of societal change, 156–157
    mindset change, 154–155
Trusts with wealth, for social purpose, 99

Uber, 212–214
Udwadia, Farrokh, 13
Uncertainty, transformation and, 61
Unfiltered leader, 80–81
    success of, 84
Unilever, 2, 54, 65, 71–72, 89, 92, 94, 99, 141, 153, 192, 195, 211, 215
Unilever Arabia, 7, 24, 49
    organisational transformation in, 26–29
Unilever Indonesia, 132
United Breweries (UB) Group of companies, 62

Urbanisation, 136–137
USA, companies and brands in, 210

Vajpayee, Atal Bihari, 45
Value-creating methodology, 190
Vanderbilt, Cornelius 'Commodore', 1
Vanderbilt: The Rise and Fall of an American Dynasty (Anderson Cooper), 1
Vanderbilt, William, 1
Vatsal, Max, 124
Venkataramani, K., 104
Victory, early declaration of, 53–54
Viehbacher, Chris, 83–84
Vietnam War, 62
Viewpoints, in organisation, 67
Voltas, 83

Walmart, 125, 150, 151
Walton, Sam, 125
Wardrobe concept, 159
War games, 132–133
Washing powders market, 195–200
Watkins, Michael, 90
Weinberg, Serge, 84
Welch, Jack, 58, 80
Who Says Elephants Can't Dance? (Louis Gerstner), 60, 83
Wi-Fi, 139
Wind turbine technology, 171
Wireless devices, 138–139
The World Is Flat (Thomas Friedman), 126
Wozniak, Steve, 221

Xerox, 132

Y2K wave, 102, 105–106
Youthfulness, corporate, 94

Zuckerberg, Mark, 140

About the Authors

R. Gopalakrishnan (Gopal) has been involved in multiple organisational transformations during his professional career of over fifty years in Unilever and in Tata. He has played multiple roles on more than twenty company boards in India and abroad. Through his rich leadership experience, he has also had a ringside seat during the period when business transformation has evolved from being episodic half a century ago to continuous in modern times.

This is Gopal's nineteenth book. He welcomes reader feedback at rgopal@themindworks.me

Hrishi Bhattacharyya is a management consultant, teacher and author. In a career spanning fifty years, he was a senior vice president in Unilever, based at their company headquarters in Europe, where he had global responsibility for the 'Health & Wellness' category. He has been a Visiting Faculty of Strategy at the Ross School of Business, University of Michigan, Ann Arbor, and has taught international business part-time at the London Business School. He is Founder/Owner of Business Strategy Consulting. He has co-authored scholarly papers with Dr C.K. Prahalad.

Hrishi has a degree with honours in economics and an MBA. He is an alumnus of the Indian Institute of Management and Harvard Business School (AMP).

6991 -